C. FAUSTO CABRERA & ALEC SOTH
THE PARAMETERS OF OUR CAGE

This book is made up of correspondence between C. Fausto Cabrera, a prisoner in the Minnesota Correctional Facility at Rush City, and Minneapolis based photographer, Alec Soth.

All proceeds from this book will be donated to the Minnesota Prison Writing Workshop mnprisonwriting.org

1.28.20

Alec Soth,

Please forgive the audacity of this letter. I reach out in great admiration and respect.

For years, I have relied on photography for reference material, given my incarceration, and have developed a great admiration for the genre. By sheer impulse, I am reaching out to local artists I admire in the hope to ignite a professional dialogue. I have no real expectation but to connect with other artists. Incarceration comes with a low glass ceiling. By no way am I absolved of my past – but I seek to pay something forward through my art and writing…

I pray to you all the duende to continue to inspire through your work…

Much Respect,
C. Fausto

2.5.20

Dear C. Fausto (or should I call you Chris?),

I'm just home from a road trip and found your recent letter awaiting me. You wrote that for years you'd used photography as reference material. I'm wondering if you could tell me more about that. Are there specific photographs you remember using? Are you able to keep printed photos in your cell? If so, what are they, and where do you keep them?

I'm particularly fascinated by the relationship of photography to the lack of freedom. Just today, I received a book in the mail by Libuše Jarcovjáková, a woman who photographed in Communist Prague in the 1970s. She writes:

Faraway places, trips, adventures... that was what really appealed to me. But the Czechoslovakia of my childhood was a country bordered by barbed wire and you weren't allowed to travel. It was a time of oppression, during which for more than 40 years we were the political vessels of a large Eastern empire. Everything was ideology, you were surrounded by political propaganda from morning to evening... Luckily, I didn't really take in my surroundings. There was a world of books and pictures and I spent hours imbibing them.

I'm wondering if there are any photographs you are particularly hungry to see. These could be photographs for your writing, or just for personal comfort. They could be of loved ones or faraway places. Is there a place you dream of traveling?

With gratitude,
Alec

2.12.20

Hey Alec,

Please allow me to give a little context to my perspective: I spent the bulk of my sentence at Stillwater working in the art department, which is the only full-time vocational studio space in the Department of Corrections [DOC]. I developed as an artist and was granted the privilege of shaping the program and managing 17-20 students with the bulk of the instructing. I wrote a curriculum that mirrored my development done mostly by independent study and experience. Our resources were limited, but looking back, relatively speaking, we were blessed with a lot of opportunities and options to order books, DVDs, and source material. Building a respectable library and materials inventory was one of my great honors. But three years ago, I was transferred to this wasteland of a prison in Rush City. My materials are reduced to a tiny personal inventory that is constantly challenged. My source material is limited to ten books and files that must fit into a 2-foot locker with all my other property. I can only have a limited number of photographs and clippings from magazines. Early on, I gravitated toward portraits, namely of women. I got incarcerated at 22, so I chased that look of allure seen in the eyes of most models, actresses, and musicians. Unbeknownst to me at the time, I just wanted to be seen.

When I was in High School, I played AAU basketball in the summer and went to Washington, D.C., for a tournament. My buddies' father told us not to waste any film on sites or monuments. He said, "pictures without people are pointless." After we returned and I had my film developed, I reflected and found that every picture taken without my friends amounted to a bad postcard. That principle always stuck with me until I started to study landscapes. It took me years to appreciate the power of a well-crafted scene. It dawned on me one day that photos without people captured the solitude of a single viewer; that there is always someone 'in' the picture. Around that same time, I started to appreciate the artistic vision of the photographer.

In Stillwater, I made collages of clippings and photographs. For years I compiled art, portraits, objects, landscapes, anything that even vaguely caught my attention. I'd collect files of the random 'inspirations' that I'd eventually cut out and fit into a puzzle of a sort — matching them only by contour to fit as many as possible on each page in a 3-ring binder. I read somewhere that creativity boils down to the ability to find the connecting threads of contradicting or otherwise separate ideas or things. Whenever I felt stuck or bored, I'd page through these volumes of binders for inspiration while letting my mind wander.

There is this fascinating duality in the concept of escapism in photography. The ability to capture the spirit of a place so fully it serves as a portal. It's so easy to romanticize it, especially when you're living a life filled with longing. In the quote you sent, it appears the woman used the materials to endure the limitations, to remind her of a broader perspective.

There's a quote by Marilynne Robinson from *Housekeeping* that says, "When do our senses know anything so utterly as when we lack it?" The Czechoslovakian photographer's childhood is defined by these "faraway places" that come alive in her longing. It is where the value of those photographs comes from, right? I mean, I'm positive whoever lived in those faraway places couldn't possibly view those landscapes in the same light. It's that interesting duality

— in our desire to escape, we turn toward what we most desire to escape in order to sharpen the vision of what we long for. This wakes us up to the artist within that must confront our fears by quantifying them somehow.

I know it's pretty early and there is so much to ask. I'm really curious about your journey as an artist. I also know we share a plight with "the darkness of depression" (hope that's not presumptuous).

Oh, you can call me Chris or Fausto. I publish under C. Fausto, but everyone knows me around here as Chris. I've acknowledged that moving forward I'll most likely go by Fausto.

Talk to you soon,
C. Fausto Cabrera

3.10.20

Dear Fausto,

I was saddened to hear about all of your restrictions at Rush City. Your predicament makes for a fascinating question: if I were only to have a 2ft locker in which to store all of my property, what would I put in there? I'm reminded of an event I did a few years ago in London in which I was asked to talk about the eight photographs I would take with me to a desert island. Of course, if this were really to be the case, I'm sure I would take pictures of loved ones. I would also want at least one picture of a woman (even at age 50, much less 22.) One of the images I chose was by a Dutch photographer named Ed Van der Elsken. It's of a beautiful woman with her leg in a cast. She stares out the window at snowy mountains while only wearing underwear. It's called "Apres Ski."

I'm always drawn to photographs with windows. For me, they speak to the quality of longing that drew me to photography in the first place. In this case, the longing of the woman to be skiing and the longing of the photographer to be in bed with the woman. Did you ever get the chance to see Hitchcock's movie *Rear Window*? Jimmie Stewart stars as a wheelchair-bound photographer who spies on his neighbors — including a sexy dancer and another woman he calls "Miss Lonelyhearts." I've always identified with his character.

I so appreciated what you said about photographs without people. One of my eight desert island pictures was taken by photographer Robert Frank as part of his book *The Americans*. It is titled "View from Hotel Window. Butte, Montana. 1955." It's an ordinary snapshot without any people. It isn't even very descriptive of Butte. This picture is less about the view than it is about Robert Frank. You can feel him standing at the window.

I had the chance to look out this very window some years ago while traveling cross country on a project called *Broken Manual*. This project started as a commission to photograph in the South. When I was in Atlanta, I remembered the story of Eric Rudolph, aka The Olympic Bomber — he was the guy that bombed the 1996 Olympics. He was identified as a suspect in 1998 but wasn't captured until 2003. The FBI had him on their 10 Most Wanted list and knew he was in the Nantahala National Forest in North Carolina, but he was a savvy enough survivalist to escape capture. I was fascinated by his years as a fugitive. So I drove to the location in North Carolina where the FBI eventually found him dumpster-diving.

On my way to that location, I happened to drive by a small Greek Orthodox monastery in Northern Georgia. I ended up photographing one of the few monks living there. He was a relatively young guy who'd been living at the monastery for years. In my mind I made a connection between him and the fugitive. While the reasons these two men left society couldn't be more different, they both sparked in me a similar longing to escape. Needless to say, yes, I do indeed battle with "the darkness of depression."

There's something from your last letter that I wrote down in my journal: "creativity boils down to the ability to find the connecting threads of contradicting or otherwise separate ideas or things." This is precisely the way it is for me: diving deep into myself and making subconscious connections. I do all sorts of research first, but it's when it settles, often in the liminal state between wakefulness and sleep, where the threads come together. It feels like magic.

I wonder if you could do something for me. Can you describe the eight photographs you might take to a desert island? These can be loved ones, magazine pictures, anything. The more detail the better.

With gratitude,
Alec

3.17.20

Hey Alec,

I hope you are negotiating this Coronavirus pandemic well enough. I know the world has not been very familiar to me for a long time, but I acknowledge how crazy it must be out there under all these restrictions and paradigm shifts. How are you handling it all? I assume you're laying low and limiting travel? The DOC shut down our visiting so far but nothing too drastic yet. I imagine we're headed for a lockdown soon.

So the worst part about my 2-bin restriction at Rush City is that my choices are even limited to an allowable property list. It all boils down to limits, huh? Whether enforced by nature — biologic or social, tangible or abstract, we all confront the parameters of our cage eventually. What we do when we reach those bars helps define us, huh.

Okay, so I'll try to attack the eight photographs in the least neurotic way I can muster. The first and easiest that came to mind is the photo of my mother I used to have. It was taken just before she got really sick. Chemo had to have just begun the second time because her hair was flat and thinning a bit. She's wearing this black t-shirt with an orange screen print of something I can't quite recall that she'd often find comfort in. She's in full profile at the height of laughter with her mouth hanging open. It's one of those pictures that makes you feel silly because it captures the essence of joy beyond ego or control; a laughing fit that makes your eyes water and damn nears steals your breath; it's so special and rare to capture. This photo was the only way I could hear my mom's laugh from in here.

She died when I was 12, which became the root of my disfunction — in hindsight of course. I'm pretty sure I still have the picture at my Aunt's house. I've had to send a lot of stuff home throughout the years. They never used to be so strict, but this facility prides itself on petty enforcements and frivolous control. So I don't keep many personal photos of loved ones any more. It's the reverse of what you'd think, I suppose. I draw comfort from the voices and visits of those still around; their photos do little to capture their essence. There is a function to nostalgia I can't necessarily afford to keep around right now given the limits to my property.

My celly is a short-timer on his second bid. He's got these four photos he keeps around him constantly: one of his son, one of him and his girl, one of just her and another of their dog. I suppose it gives him comfort to keep his focus on his family unit still close enough to serve as a tangible inspiration. I find him engulfed in them often, which makes me believe he might be on a better track in life.

Picture #2 — The next easiest one is a setting. When my mom died, my Aunt Kathy & Uncle Steve took us (me, sister (+2 yrs) & brother (-8yrs) into their home. Her two kids were already out of the house. Steve was always my father figure and the reason I never hated my dad for never being around. They lead our family unit from the projects of Joliet and Rockford, IL, into the middle class suburbs of MN. They bought some property in Isanti, sold it to developers then upgraded to a 10-acre hobby farm around the corner from the old place. It's been their dream to invest in this property. I got locked up in 2003 and saw it at a certain stage of development, but they have done so much to it since. Kathy's daughter had eight kids — when I went away, they became foster parents to all eight!

My Aunt had her first child at 15 and has been raising children her whole life. I think she's addicted to children; there's an open-door policy so the grandchildren are always around. So the second photo would be a summer's day of the property that'd capture the scope of the place while everyone is outside — like you couldn't make out too much detail — more of a figurative touch. As you'd approach the place from the road, with enough of the sky and surrounding nature to capture the outdoorsy element of the landscape.

This really is a question of the value of photography, huh? By having to choose eight, I really have to confront many aspects of myself and what's important to me. Please allow me to step outside the bounds of the spirit of the question to comment as a man of personal limitation to joke in seriousness: if this was for real, for real all eight would be porn!! Haha! Porn was outlawed in the early 2000s and a strict "nudity" policy is heavily enforced. The true torture of a man is to criminalize his sexuality. When women are treated as objects to be taken away, we are taught to objectify them. So, needless to say, spending my 20s & 30s incarcerated has heightened my appreciation for everything feminine. I have tried to err on the side of appreciation. So I'd say pictures 3-8 will rely on a female presence.

I was thinking about how some different categories might merge to pack as many needs and desires into one photo. Like trying to think back to nostalgic images of my youth. Something like the Tyra Banks swimsuit edition of Sports Illustrated or the first Playboy I could remember. For some reason, the Charolette Lewis edition sticks with me because I loved her in Eddie Murphy's movie *The Golden Child*. But the more I think about the past in these terms, the more detached I feel. It'd be a waste to reach in my memory as opposed to desire something new. What does that say about me? Do I lack appreciation of the past, or is it a residual effect of living with such regret?

#3 — I went to school behind local weatherman Dave Dahl's son DJ. We used to play ball together and DJ was a positive influence on me. He got me a shot at playing b-ball at MCTC [Minneapolis Community and Technical College] when my options dried up. One day we're riding in DJ's car and all he has is women singers: Tori Amos, Alanis Morissette, etc. All I listened to was rap and "tough guy" shit at the time, so I started messing with him about his selection. Then he broke down his perspective that forever changed my music palette. "Bro, why would I want to listen to dudes? I want to hear a female and feel like she's pouring her broken heart right at my feet. I want to believe she's calling out directly to me and praying that I save her." It's the governing idea behind the portraits of the females I'm drawn to — that personal connection pulling me into those eyes staring into my desiccated soul. So there are a few females that have cried out to me and shared my pain throughout my bid: Lana Del Rey, Halsey, K.Flay & Maria Brink. All of these women hold a certain darkness within that I instantly related to. I'd say #3 would be any one of them caught in some sort of seductive poster-like pose, letting me know I'm not alone while I listen to their songs.

#4 — There is one singer that has recently haunted me. Demi Lovato's songs "Anyone" & "Tell Me You Love Me" have brought me to tears with the feeling of shared solitude. So #4 is more of a collaboration. It'd be Demi in a cluttered room, messy like a teenager's, not dirty but more like lived in. I'd want her to pepper the room with personal items: photos, notebooks, talismans infused with their own nostalgia, things I could pore over to figure out what they say about her journey. On the wall along with whatever she has are three posters spaced out: Guns & Roses' *Appetite for Destruction* album cover, Che Guevera's picture smoking a cigar – somewhat well-groomed with a jovial look on his face – and Tupac Shakur in the BMW right before he got shot up in Vegas. In the corner of the room is a life-size skeleton (that's for my drawing reference). I'd want to catch her completely immersed in writing a song wearing just an oversized shirt with her hair messily up. Preferably it'd catch enough of her face to be able to understand the anatomy of her features, possibly 3/4 profile.

Have you heard of Suicide Girls? Pin-up tattooed models. A lot of them are nude, so my scope is limited, but because I'm a tattooer (well, amateur prison tattooer), I'm transfixed by beautiful women wearing good art. The pin-up genre has always been a magnet for men going off to war or littered on walls of solitude. So this answer is aspirational in its conception. I've been designing original tattoos for years for guys around here and I've done a few for my cousins, but my goal is to find my own suicide girls. Since I can't tattoo women from in here, I'm trying to share my portfolio with tattooers out there, until I get out and tattoo on my own. So #5-6 will be "my Suicide Girls."

#7 – I am certainly at peace in my solitude, but it also has me thinking about breaking out of it at moments. The longest I have ever been to segregation was for 45 days. When I got out back into the general prison population, it was the strangest feeling. I suppose it's like when people go camping in remote places, or even car trips, which you've touched upon when articulating the distance you feel between yourself and other people. When I got out of isolation, I felt changed, and crowds took on a new meaning and developed a different feel. Everyone will know what I mean when the pandemic settles. There's a line between my desire to be around certain specific people and my curiosity to meet new people – or to find more of "my people". So I'm thinking the next photo would be faces in a crowd, like a well-lit bar, or maybe a march or protest, which is interesting in context considering this Coronavirus pandemic. I think I'd want #7 to be strangers in a packed setting.

#8 – a photo of cell 405 in A-West at Stillwater; a place I've spent a lot of time in. It makes me think about the Czech woman you referenced in your earlier letter. She said, "I didn't really take in my surroundings." I think there is a debt we owe to our suffering, or to the source of our longings. Art as pure escapism is valuable, but there is a point where it can become delusion. I'd want this photo for a few complicated reasons. On the surface, it's about never forgetting. More importantly, it'd be a testament of my existence. Knowing this photo exists would remind me that it wasn't all in vain. There is a complexity to my life I can never forget. Getting out isn't the end of my prison sentence; it's the beginning of my true redemption. My supposed debt to society in a cage doesn't account for my debt to humanity.

Much Respect,
Fausto

4.6.20

Dear Fausto,

It is such a pleasure receiving your letters. I have to say this whole Coronavirus situation has altered the way I think about our correspondence. I'm profoundly aware of the fact that "shelter in place" bears zero resemblance to what you face each day, lockdown or not. And lest you think I romanticize prison, I assure you I don't. Or at least don't try to. For as long as I can remember, my biggest fear has been prison. But this has less to do with the isolation than the social dynamic, the various power structures, the abuse. I couldn't survive it.

One interesting thing about being a photographer is that it has allowed me to explore this fear. During the making of my first book, *Sleeping by the Mississippi*, I visited Angola State Prison in Louisiana — the largest maximum-security facility in the US. It is surrounded by the Mississippi on three sides and was a former slave plantation. The picture I took in 2002 of African American inmates working the fields while white officers patrolled on horseback looks like it could have been made 150 years ago. In the years since I've visited several other prisons. I photographed a man on death row, a hitman in Michigan, the prison in Arkansas where Leadbelly recorded in the 1930s, and the aftermath of an execution in Huntsville, Texas.

Is there anywhere you'd like to travel when you get out — in the US or abroad? Currently I'm not traveling because of Covid19. It is such a peculiar time. I belong to an agency called Magnum Photos. It is a co-operative created by a few photographers after WWII. There are approximately 50 photographers in the agency. They live all over the world and travel relentlessly. Many of them photograph wars and global conflicts. But during this pandemic, all but a couple are staying at home. As a consequence, a group email chain was created. People are sharing their pictures from home. But I've had trouble responding. Over the years, I've tried a couple of times to photograph my family and our domestic life, but it never feels right. Many of my favorite photographers do this sort of work. It is so beautiful. And meaningful. I think of your description of the photograph of your mother laughing. There's nothing more human than that kind of image. But something in me resists doing such personal work.

I've found that I have to go out into the world to take pictures, but my goal is always to explore an internal place simultaneously. *Sleeping by the Mississippi* barely has a photo of the river; it's about my desire to wander. My next book, tentatively titled *A Box of Pictures*, is both about photography and my psychological need to interact with the world from behind a lens.

Selfishly, this is why I keep asking you questions about photography. You are so thoughtful, Fausto, and your perspective is so refreshing. This new project isn't just about fine art photography. I'm interested in all the ways we use photos, from snapshots to porn. The way you imagine pictures with such vivid detail is possible because you have the imagination of an artist whose creativity has been affected by the constraints of your incarceration. I've been holding onto these words of yours: "We all confront the parameters of our cage eventually. What we do when we reach those bars helps define us."

In the wake of the coronavirus, a magazine contacted me saying, "Now that we find ourselves in this situation, we've begun to think of people who, like yourself, may be more used to this more isolated experience of day to day life. People that almost actively search it out, whether it be for personal reasons or creative." Before I pass along what I wrote, I want to share what the magazine posted by a Tunisian artist named Rafram Chaddad. Ten years ago, while traveling through Libya, he was kidnapped by the Libyan secret police and held for six months in prison. He wrote:

Surprisingly, during my 170 days of solitary confinement, I learnt that it's easier to have inner thoughts when you're alone. And not only without people, but alone without any triggers that push you to think outside of yourself... I managed to live a full and interesting life without anything, because the radical situation I was in pushed me to go inside my dreams and live daily — day after day — a rich, crazy, and wonderful life. With the help and comfort of the temptations around us, we are alienated from ourselves.

I'm embarrassed to send you what I wrote. I've never been in a situation like that — and certainly nothing like yours. As I said, I come from a privileged background. I grew up in Chanhassen. At the time it was in the country. My big claim to fame is that Prince lived very close by (before he moved into Paisley Park). But I never met him. It was a charming old farmhouse with lots of land. My dad was a lawyer and I was lucky to have a stable home, financially and otherwise. But I was always a weirdo. I was shy and had some traumatic stuff happen when I was young. So I kept to myself. This expressed itself in peculiar ways — I had pretend friends and a kind of creative universe as a kid. In high school a teacher recognized this as creativity, not just weirdness, and opened up a path for me. At first this was through painting. But I never felt authentic doing that. Eventually, I found my way to photography.

Anyway, this is what I wrote for the magazine:

One can be a connoisseur of anything. In the late 90s, when the internet was new, I interviewed an Israeli man who was a connoisseur of women's fingernails — he deemed himself 'the father of fingernail fetish photography'. Though I didn't share his interest, I asked if I could acquire an appreciation. After a couple of weeks of taking pictures of fingernails, I wouldn't say I became an aficionado, but I started to develop an eye.

Susan Sontag called the flâneur a "connoisseur of empathy" and considered photographers to be "an armed version of the solitary walker… the voyeuristic stroller who discovers the city as a landscape of voluptuous extremes". While this might be true of someone like Weegee, there are many types of photographic connoisseurship.

What kind of photographer are you? How I dread that question. While I've never wished to be a wedding photographer, at least it would give me a reasonable answer. When I'm asked this question, more often than not by a fellow traveler before I have the chance to feign interest in the inflight magazine, I usually mutter something about making portraits along the Mississippi River. "Like National Geographic?" they sometimes reply. I imagine Susan Sontag overhearing this in the row behind me and rolling her eyes. But I've never claimed to be a connoisseur of empathy. Nor do I profess to know much about the Mississippi River and its inhabitants. I often say that when I take a portrait, the thing I'm really capturing is the space between myself and my subject. If I'm a connoisseur of anything, it's social distance.

My appreciation of distance has come in handy the last couple of months. While I'd never heard the term 'social distancing' until now, it's a concept that comes naturally to me. Over many years of observing people while hidden under a camera dark cloth, I've rarely come closer than the new six-foot health guidelines. My ideal distance for making a portrait is about the length of a seesaw — close enough to exchange energy, but far enough to properly visualize separateness.

What advice can I share for the countless people learning to live with the new social restrictions? Try to look at social space the way a sommelier looks at wine. Swirl it in the light. You needn't intoxicate yourself in loneliness, just hold it to your nose and breathe.

I'm self-conscious about sending you this text because it is so clearly written from the vantage point of someone with extraordinary freedom. The "stay at home" orders for someone with a house and yard in South Minneapolis are different than for someone in a crowded apartment building in Queens, much less someone on lockdown in prison.

What's fascinating in talking to you is how those limitations alter one's creative path. I've always believed that my creativity has its roots in my lonely childhood. And I have the sense that your creative sensibility has been hugely affected by your childhood as well as your incarceration.

Your description of your eight desert island photographs was remarkable. Such vivid detail! I loved your description of the Demi Lovato photograph. So I came up with an idea. On Instagram I created a contest. I said I would send one of my signed photographs to the person who created the best Photoshop version of this picture. From over forty submissions, I chose five finalists.

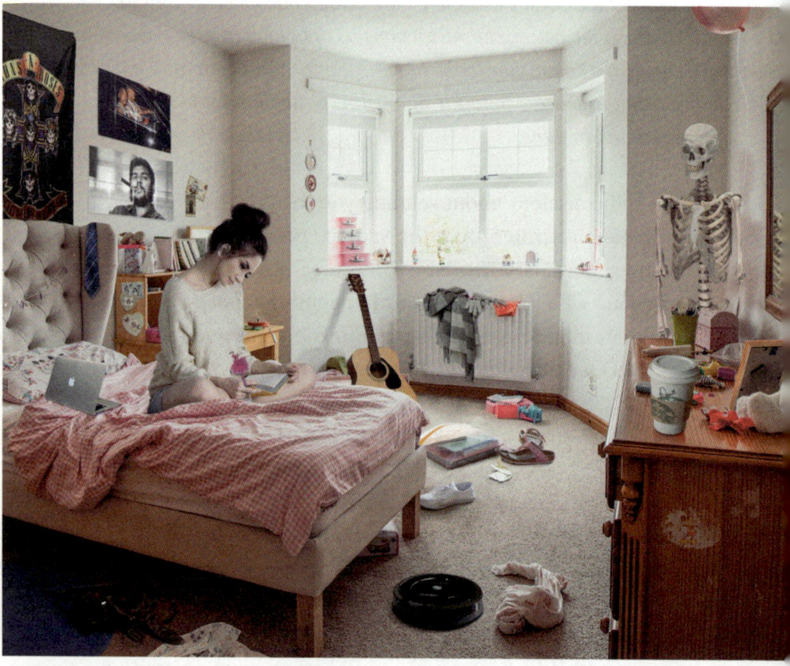

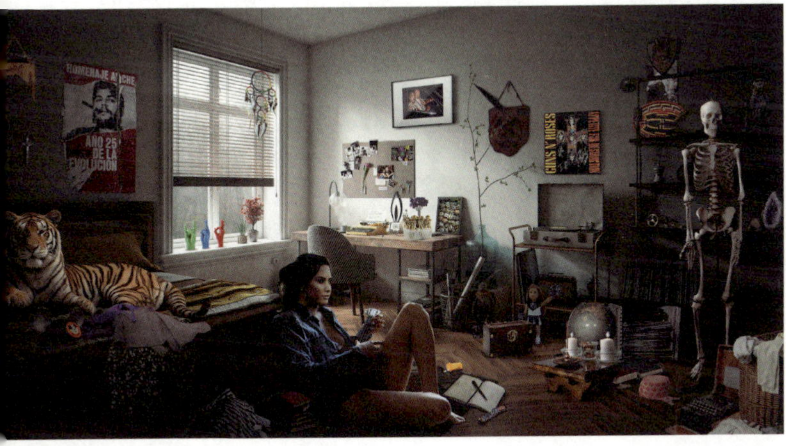
HOMENAJE A CHE
AÑO 25
DE LA
GUNS N' ROSES

GUNS N' ROSES
Live
Laugh
Love
Say it to my face.
Not through
your status.
TEEN
CHOICE
2014
JACOB

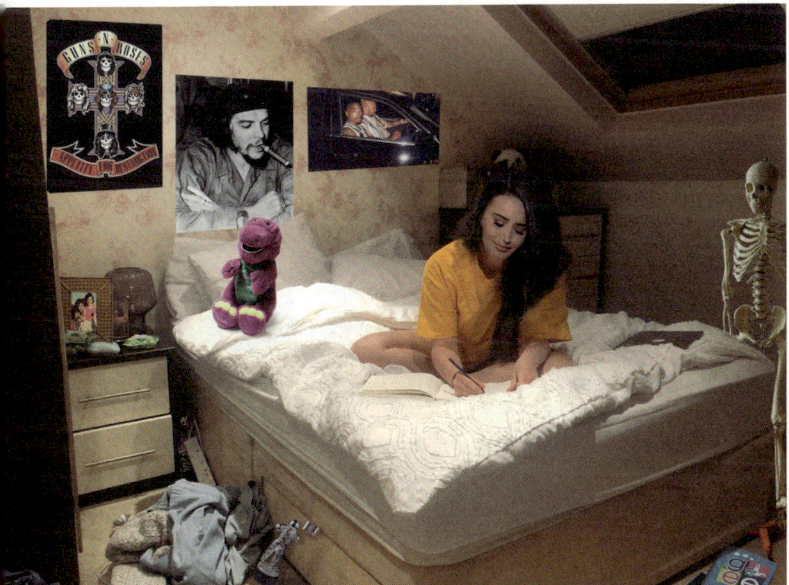
GUNS N ROSES
glee

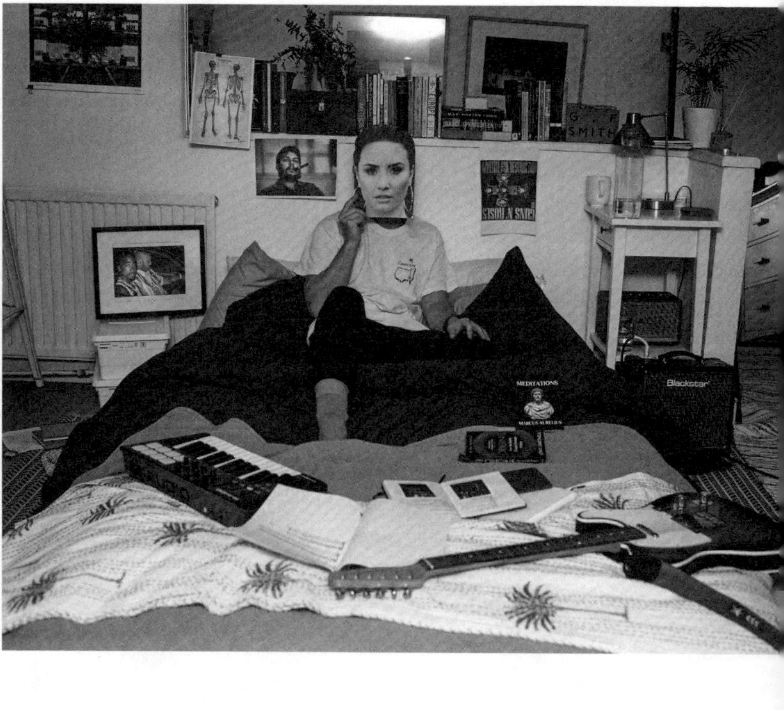
MEDITATIONS
MARCUS AURELIUS
Blackstar
G F
SMITH

I'm curious to see which you like the best!

Okay my friend. I hope that your spirits are okay. I'm so grateful for your friendship.

All my best,
Alec

4.10.20

Dear Alec,

Man, the Demi challenge is awesome. I am honored and so impressed by the extent of your effort to make my words tangible. There is a certain magic of possibility in this gesture. I am over the moon! My clear winner is #2. It's a great combination of sexiness and shadows. And the fierceness of the tiger is an awesome touch. I feel like this is the photo that most focuses on the connective thread that bonds artist to artist, and more of a collaboration — which was the spirit of the vision.

#1 & 3 take a brighter approach. I admit that this might personify Demi's image possibly better than how I see her because I am not able to do much research. I think what draws us to art is the depth of reflection. The more we see ourselves, the stronger the connection – idealized or otherwise. Each and every one is great in their own right. That's awesome you did this Alec, thanks again.

I hope you and yours are in good spirits during these days, staying healthy and occupying your minds. I liked how you quantified your work and saw it in such terms – a connoisseur of distance. I never really thought about carrying around solitude like you've described. Solitude's done me well in the Rilke "Letters to a Young Poet" sense. My incarceration has honed my craft and heightened my artistic senses, and I imagine I'll always carry that solitude with me when I get out. There is a strong connective thread between us. I love that awareness you have of it: "close enough to exchange energy, but far enough to properly visualize separateness."

I am certain you would have been alright in prison, Alec. There is an elasticity to the human soul you never confront until it's stretched. The politics and abuse are exhausting, but oddly it's the thing that's easiest to endure. The physical part (the lack of female companionship aside) is nothing compared to the cerebral and emotional scarring. It's funny how photography has allowed you to explore your fear of prison. Whereas you went that way, I ran toward death and prison because of my personal brokenness. We've responded to the darkness in different ways and here we are – our paths converged.

Travel is an interesting subject. I'm not sure what is possible. I know that when I am on parole, I'll have to get permission to cross state borders, let alone leave the country. I don't want to invest in daydreams of travel if it's not possible. It's like – if I know I can't have my own experience, it's frivolous to think about a place for that place's sake. I can appreciate the value, but my focus is on relationships and experiences. Like, I guess I'd like to visit Peru's Amazon but more to partake in an Ayahuasca ceremony. My Afro-Cuban dad was the only one to defect from Cuba. I have his sister's address in Guantanamo. But since I don't speak Spanish and they don't speak English, letters are tough. I guess we've got family in Havana too.

You asked about my old cell. I spent the bulk of my time in Stillwater over in unit A-West. Of the four tiers, the top two, 15 cells from the end was like our neighborhood. We could control who lived where so that section was a type of "gated community". 405 was my cell for years, and when it wasn't, one of my brothers was in it. Years ago we were able to screw the bolts off of the vents at the back of the cells which gave us access to the long enclosed space where we could hide a hooch brewing operation. I used to tattoo in that cell too.

Stillwater has an open bar system similar to Alcatraz; only it faces the wall. When guards do rounds, they walk up and down the tiers in pairs every hour. When you were doing anything illegal, you must have a team of "spotters" to alert you quickly enough not to get caught. When it was time to pull a batch of hooch from the vents there was a small window of opportunity, we had to treat it as a pit crew because it was loud and you could smell it from 50 feet away. The stakes seemed high when you are looking forward to drinking with your buddies to decompress.

So much time in prison is fraternal. We're in our 20-30s just trying to figure out what we should be doing. We had to take our limitations with a grain of salt and figure it all out. Many years became about flag football championships and softball titles. At least a few times a year some weed came through and it'd make things smoother. Without lighters or papers we'd have to get creative by smoking out of apples and lighting fires on Q-Tips from electrical outlets. The whole process had to be efficient because, like the hooch, there is a small window of opportunity. Most of us had more than twenty years to serve. We were still going to college and participating in programming, but this was our life now. Mostly, we needed distraction. Our incarceration was supposed to be the solution. Surviving a terrible place isn't justice; it's a waste of resources. Prison is a terrible place by design with a dark purpose. But just like foxholes, they become places that mold relationships and character through the resiliency of those that find ways to make it through the wars. Since they were single cells, it was easy to make it your home. You could spend decades in a unit or a certain cell. Here in Rush City, it's double-bunked and unstable — there is no space to ever feel grounded here. Sadly, Stillwater is like a home to me more than anywhere else.

I am the tale of two cities straddling the fence with one foot on the green grass of the suburbs and one foot on the cracked concrete of Minneapolis. Whether I was the token minority around upper-middle-class white kids or cousin Chris from the suburbs who was light yellow and enunciated his words like an outsider, my family was climbing the social ladder, but we were still outlaws. We didn't call the police, we called in Uncle Steve when there were issues. He kept guns and was the natural patriarch. I was raised in this amalgamation of cultures; sports, streets, hip-hop, Cuban crimewave, good schools, a whole spectrum of diverse friends, etc. We find our identity in the influences around us at an age where we can't possibly process any of it in an objective or stable manner. I love how you said it was a high school teacher that recognized your 'weirdness' as creativity and how it set you on a path. I had good people around me, mixed in with a lot of skewed perspectives and emotionally charged experiences. I had plenty of opportunities to follow some good paths, and I almost did. It's funny because the positive influences are still around, my Uncle Steve, my High School basketball coach; even through all of my bullshit they still believe in me.

My mother's death amplified the darkness already growing inside of me. I was able to bury a lot of my demons deep down by engaging in sports. I dabbled in art but never really thought of it as a tangible career possibility for some reason. I'd roof and side houses with Steve for cash in the summers in between playing basketball. When I graduated in '99, I went down to the cities with my cousin with the hopes to play ball at MCTC where DJ introduced me to the coach. If I had applied myself more, I could have gone to a small college on a scholarship, but I didn't work hard enough. My depression was crippling. I didn't understand it as such at the time, but it caused me to live passively, just going with a flow – floating down a river of whoever came into my life. For some reason, I didn't want to take out student loans or be in debt, so when the grants I applied for didn't cover books, I dropped out. I look back and kick myself for failing to comprehend the ultimate value of a life within my reach. I just allowed myself to drift.

I met a girl in Minneapolis who mesmerized me with her dysfunction. It was mainly physical at first, but quickly became a perfect storm of challenge, toxicity, and codependence. I moved in with her and her parents for a while and disappeared in a minimalist mentality of survival where finding a blunt to smoke was the daily goal. Everyone else could see it so I stayed away from my family and lost myself. We got an apartment and I began to climb out of my depression with her attached to my hip. Her dysfunction made me feel like the 'normal' one. I refurbished houses with a small company during the real estate boom, which taught me how to do everything from framing, kitchens, bathrooms, electrical, and plumbing. They'd buy crack houses and bring them up to code then sell them. After a few years of that I went on my own and started subcontracting residentially. Because I've always had one foot in and one foot out of the streets, I started flipping cocaine and weed while building my tools and gun collection. I developed an odd resentment toward my girl for all of the bullshit I felt she put me through and instead of confronting it I did whatever I wanted, going out to bars and cheating. I started hanging out with her big brother who was recently released from prison for a drug trafficking case. In the span of a few years, I just didn't care about the trajectory of my life. I was engulfed in a violent culture where you accepted you might get shot every time you left the house. I carried a gun because I had bought into the necessity of it. I'd be damned if someone tried to stick me up, or the police were going to shoot me for nothing. You look back on your perception when in your early 20s or late teens and can't remember exactly why you felt certain ways. It's easy to see how stupid and pointless it seems from the outside when looking back or from an elevated perspective. Throw a deep-seated depression in the mix and it's easier than it seems to get swept up in the unmanageable current.

One night, I'm drunk and high and I go into the Stardust bar (now Memory Lanes) with my dirtbag big brother and get into a fight over some girl. I'm too arrogant to realize I'm being disrespectful, in a bar where the security is an on-duty South Minneapolis police officer. I assume full responsibility for my actions, Alec. I never want the reasons for my actions to be conveyed as excuses, but things didn't happen in a vacuum either. The officer maced me directly and kicked everyone out of the bar at the same time, essentially lighting the fuse on a powder keg. I didn't know if they had a gun, but I knew I had one. All my rage and darkness was oozing anger and adrenaline and I let my girl's big brother spin me like a top, like a little devil on my shoulder — I flushed everything down the toilet. I recklessly shot up their car. The man who had the least to do with it was killed. It was all bad.

I knew time was running out, so I got on a Greyhound with a backpack and headed south. I made it to Corpus Christi, Texas, and rented a room with some illegals. I was almost to the border, one bus from Brownsville. I bought this book about divination that Napoleon used, a method of prayer and action where you'd meditate and then make marks until you felt the need to stop. You'd count them and it'd refer you to an answer in the book. I did it and it said that my family was worried about me and I should reach out to them. I don't know, there was a pull. I thought about my Coach and Uncles, men who raised me to be better than them. Men who believed in me. I decided to go back home.

When we pulled into Minneapolis, the weather was perfect, a bright sun gleaming off the buildings, the city had never been so beautiful, everything will work itself out accordingly. I met my Uncles, said our goodbyes, and turned myself in.

Running away is easy to glamorize, I suppose, and I often wonder what was waiting for me had I continued across the border. I'd like to think it's all part of a purpose – something connected to this duty I feel today, but I don't know, Alec. Maybe it was just mere stupidity because I wasn't done making bad decisions.

Initially I received a life sentence plus ten years. I got on the stand and lied in an attempt to contradict my co-defendant's lies. I was still thinking selfishly and hadn't owned up to how far I'd fallen. A few years later, I won my Supreme Court appeal because the prosecutor brought race into the issue. I got a chance to take a deal, so I signed for 2nd-degree murder. They gave me 4 first degree attempted murder charges for everyone in the car, adding 10 years to the sentence. As of right now, my release date is 2030.

I now take on the responsibility of owning my past fully. I know that my incarceration in and of itself has done little to solve any of the issues of crime, but it has molded me into the person I should have been all along. I believe the greatest thing we have to offer humanity is ourselves, our perceptions, our stories – our art. And I hope all of my failures qualify me to pay something forward on an insurmountable debt.

Thank you for seeing value in me and opening up your thoughts, work and heart to me. I pray you and yours are safe and in good spirits! Stay safe and wash your hands :)

Much love and respect,
Fausto

4.25.20

Dear Fausto,

I'm grateful that you told me the Memory Lanes story. I wanted to hear about it, but I don't want that story to define my understanding of you. When talking to students, I often discuss something I call "the sentence" — the shorthand people use to describe someone. "She's that Jewish poet who killed herself" for Sylvia Plath, for example. We all do this outside of creative circles, of course. A guy I work with is 6'7". He's invariably described as "that tall guy". It has to be annoying. But it would be far worse to have that sentence defined by one's mistakes or misfortune. We don't have control over our own sentence. It is formed by so many different factors: ethnicity, class, gender, and an endless web of nature, nurture, and dumb luck. But I think we can gently nudge this sentence — for ourselves and each other. It might be the case that your sentence will include your incarceration, but I don't think it has to be defined by the event that brought you there. Reginald Dwayne Betts's sentence is "the ex-con poet," not "the carjacker who writes poetry." That's not to say it's not a part of his story, it is, but it needn't be the headline. I respect how you own your story. The story of the shooting is compelling, of course, but I'm just as interested in your aunt and uncle's farm and brewing hooch in the vents. You are a storyteller, and, for me, that is more essential to your "sentence" than your crime.

As I've mentioned, I've been working on a project about photography. Along with taking pictures all over the country, I've been collecting found photographs. I've also been writing. This has been a way for me to process the way photographs — my own and others — function in the world. During the pandemic, I haven't been doing work on this project. I was supposed to go on a road trip but, of course, it was canceled. I've tried doing little things, but it hasn't been going anywhere. I've been far more interested in talking to you. I was utterly fascinated by the way you wrote about the eight photographs you'd take to a desert island — the amount of detail and the reasoning behind these choices. I love the way you weave your own experience into the way you talk about art.

So I came up with a creative exercise. My idea is to send you some snapshots I found. I'd like you to choose one or more and write about them individually. Think of the photograph as a diving board and then jump into a pool of thoughts.

Thanks, my friend…
Alec

5.6.20

Dear Alec,

Happy May to you my friend! I hope you are surrounded by love & creative verve.

One of the pictures you sent got denied because of "gang signs"? I appealed the decision, although I'm not confident in any oversight. They've denied babies holding their hands at odd angles as gang signs. Even if it is a "gang sign", who cares!? How is that a threat to security?

My initial response to these found snapshots was to breeze through and disregard them as belonging to others. It wasn't noble, like out of respect for their privacy. Rather like an absence of desire to see anyone outside of my own sphere. What's the value of personal photos unless you know the people within them? – I thought initially.

My aunt Kathy was just telling me about how she was sifting through her cardboard box of old photos and found some of me as a child. This prompted a few memories, but without seeing the specific photos I felt a bit dissociated to this inheritance coming from a box I had yet to sort. If I were to pick up a handful of photos from my family's box, each one would be electrified by bias, saturated in complicated emotion. It made me think about what you said about your aversion to taking personal pictures and the value of the distance between you and your subjects.

Thinking about that, I went through the snapshots you sent again and felt myself pulled closer. Maybe the relative distance allowed me to confront my story a little less tainted? Like when a painting has become overwhelmed with attention or an essay is too fresh with emotion. Our relationship with the past is too personal, so we put it in a box and ask time to intervene. It's interesting to enter the past by the backdoor of other people's photos.

Is the emotional connection to innocence lost forever at a certain point? Is this what nostalgia means? When we look at these types of photos is it possible to truly occupy dual points on our timeline and reclaim some innocence? We may not be able to reject cynicism, but can we choose to block some of the bitterness that's calcified our spirit to regain some of the carelessness of childhood? I see it in this snapshot, a suspension of disbelief that makes our approach to life like watching a magic trick: you must buy into the illusion in order to be swept up in the wonderment. Surrounded by family, she's blindfolded and playing some sort of absurd game, buying into the fun. Anonymously outside the frame those around her toggle through a gamut of perspectives seen through their posture: the kid at the top left corner leans on elbows anxiously at the edge ready to do something, the older lady next to her, barefoot and about to strike up a cigarette, seems to be managing the issues of the younger one who is seemingly exhausted in her own drama, while the girl in red sits fully in the chair, her body making contact at every point, on the precipice of her adulthood, and the lady on the couch with her legs crossed enjoys the show from a seasoned age.

How long has it been since I was willing to play the fool and abandon my seriousness? To shed my petty misgivings, put the blindfold on and get on my hands and knees in a position to be laughed at by people who've known me all my life? The time will arrive for her soon where she will discover things about her family she never knew, things that will change the way she may think about them. She'll start

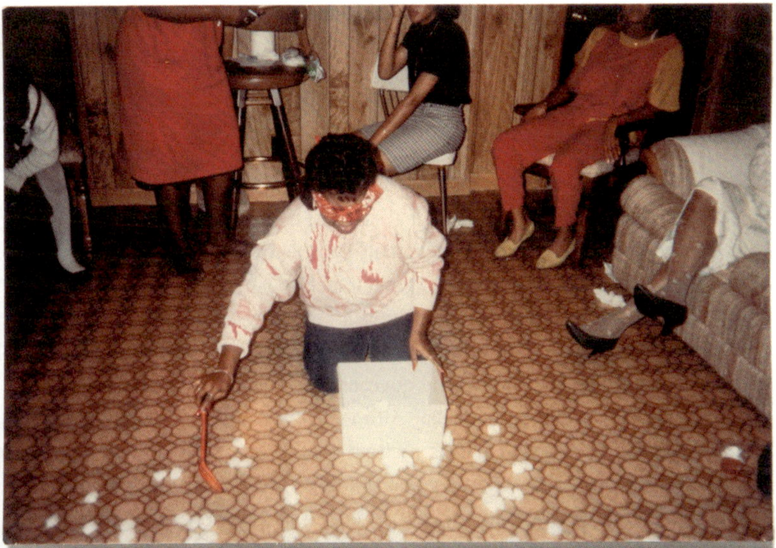

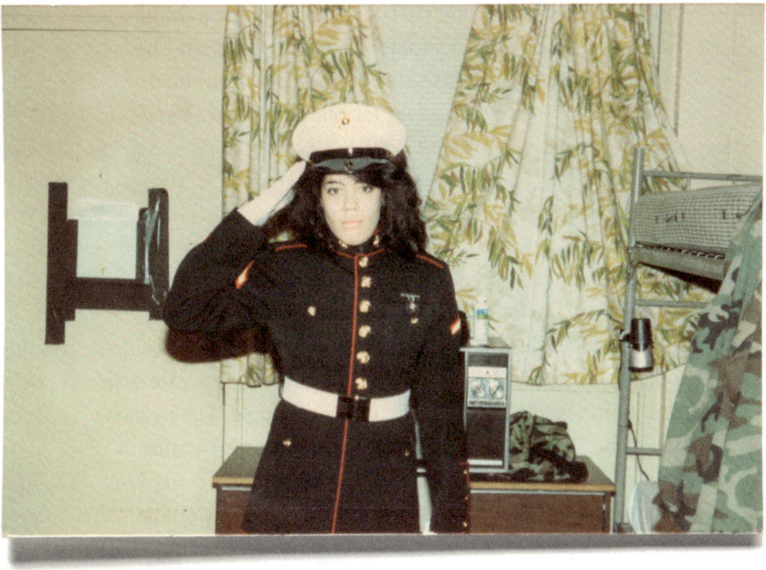

making her own adult decisions that will sacrifice degrees of her innocence and complicate the relationships that ripple around her.

When was the last time I bought into the magic of life? Without looking for the strings, calling out flaws and faults or filling the air with my cynicism? What's the big deal with putting on that blindfold and playing the fool? I'm so afraid of being taken for a fool. I've forgotten how good it feels to let go. I contemplated enlisting after high school. I vividly recall sitting in my truck as my big cousin talked me out of it. "You'd be pimpin' yourself out to the government," he said, "they don't give a fuck about us." Although I was selling him crack at the time, I felt he made a good point. Since my uncles were tax-evading construction workers, my cousins used and sold drugs, my mom smoked weed and used to hang around Cubans who personified Tony Montana from *Scarface*, I never considered the system ever to have our best interests in mind. To become a cop or join the military would've been an intentional deviation and be considered a betrayal. We saw ourselves as untrained soldiers in the streets fighting for our American Dream of money, power and respect.

It's all part of buying into that same illusion of a childhood magic trick. Despite the details of allegiance, culture or environment, the base mold of a person capable of using violence against another for whatever reason is similar. Every soldier has their justifications. The police feel entitled because their violence is sanctioned and they operate with immunity, even when they kill unarmed people. The military goes into foreign countries with a license to kill because politicians gave them permission. I grew up believing I had a right to defend myself and didn't ask for permission because I wasn't the only one with a gun on the streets.

The question becomes how we view the righteousness of the purpose. I'm not trying to justify violence or discredit law or military enforcement; I'm merely looking for solidarity with this soldier.

When I was young, life was a river I was barreled down in a boat I didn't buy, with people I didn't choose, seeing banks I didn't feel I had access to. I wonder about people who are born into law enforcement or military families or soldiers across continents who are birthed in warzones. Aren't they operating from similar ideologies? Isn't the spirit of the things we do more universal and not as black and white as a right or wrong based on a government's permission?

I know we got a few irons in the fire, but I meant to ask you more about the enlightenment you experienced on that beach. I've been struggling with depression my whole life and have recently felt more at peace than ever before. Do you think art, purpose, and maybe fine-tuning craft could somehow help to re-wire our brains and turn these shadowed elements into a function as opposed to seeing them as an illness or dysfunction? I can't even imagine who I'd be without my ability to see in my dark — all the beauty I've discovered!

Okay my friend, stay enveloped in love & blessings. I am so thankful for you.

With Love,
Fausto

5.24.20

Dear Fausto,

Sorry it took me a while to reply to your postcard and letters. I ended up traveling to Chicago for the *New York Times*. The story was about income inequality in American cities. I photographed in one neighborhood in which the average life expectancy is 90 and another where it is 60. It was a challenging assignment for all sorts of reasons, but foremost, of course, was the pandemic. I've wanted to ask you how Rush City is handling things. There are so many nightmarish stories in the news about Coronavirus in prisons.

I've been doing a lot of reflecting on our correspondence. I so appreciated your honesty when you asked, "What's the value of personal photos unless you know the people within them?" It reminds me of when you said you couldn't invest in daydreams of travel if it's not necessarily possible. What matters is your experience, your dreams, your life. The peculiar thing about me is the way I use other people's lives to learn about my own. I've probably mentioned this before, but I don't take serious photographs of my family. I can't seem to do it. Photography is a tool for me to explore the world while always preserving a certain amount of distance. It's like I'm a deep-sea diver in one of those old-fashioned diving suits. I drive around in the bubble of my minivan looking for treasure. Behind the safety of my camera, I drop into the sea, exhilarated, but not of it — octopus tentacles slapping against my lens. None of this works at home. It's clumsy and unnatural, like scuba diving in a swimming pool. I know I'm free just to wear trunks and take a relaxing swim, but it's just not me.

This is all to say that I understand this isn't natural for you. Looking at a random snapshot of women playing some sort of game in a basement isn't the first way you'd normally come to learn anything about yourself. But I appreciate that you gave it such serious effort and got something out of it. This relates to that picture that prison removed from my last letter. Here is a censored version of it.

The reason I sent you this was I thought it might connect a little bit with the Demi Lovato bedroom pictures. I also wondered if it might prompt thoughts on the presentation of toughness, which relates not only to gangs and prison but social life in general. But why talk about this through an anonymous photo? Why not go straight to the source?

I've been thinking about how much I'd love to see photographs of you and your family. Would you be okay with that? Could I contact your Aunt Kathy?

I just realized I didn't answer the questions in your last letter. I guess I'm reserving thoughts on "the new normal". It's just so hard to predict. Along with the job I did in Chicago, I recently shot a small story on a property rights group near Lake and Hiawatha. These are low-income folks, often undocumented, who brilliantly fought a slum lord and eventually purchased his property. It was a meaningful job and felt good to do something locally. I wonder if I'll be doing more local jobs. I also wonder if I'll find a way to do more of my personal work locally — but, as I've said, this is something I've struggled with. We'll just see what happens. Like so many others, I'm just sort of waiting.

Regarding your questions about "the enlightenment you experienced on the beach" — it's funny, I can't even remember telling you about that. I've looked at copies of my

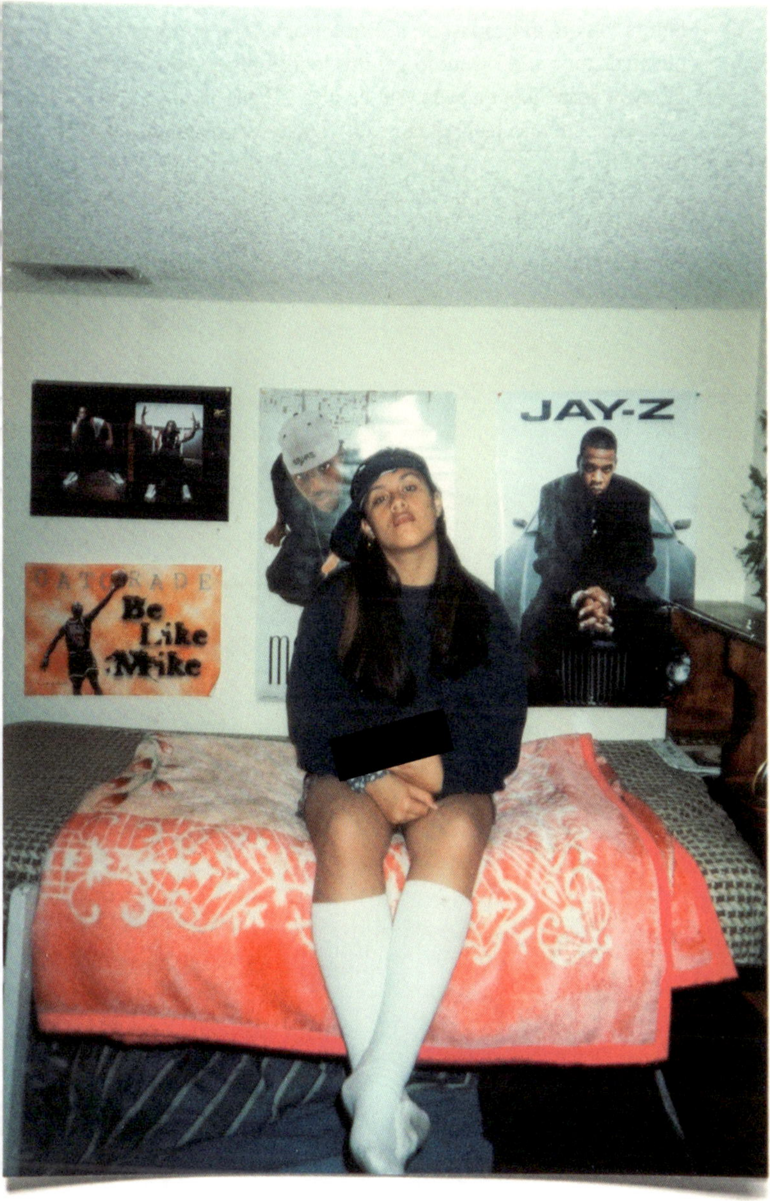
JAY-Z
Be Like Mike

letters to you and can't find it. But this is a long and complicated story and I want to get this letter out to you now. I'll try to write about it soon. But I'd love to hear more about the peace you are feeling. How do you see art playing a role with that?

Your friend,
Alec

5.30.20

Hey Alec,

I hope you are safe and are well in the midst of this new level of chaos during these protests. How are you? I've been glued to the coverage as I assume most are and have such mixed emotions. I'm both impressed and discouraged by what I'm hearing and seeing. I've never felt protected by the system. And now as a ward of the State, I see the continued failures of those who assume responsibility when it's convenient. I don't know Alec, but the problems are real and real solutions are a long time coming. How are you processing all of this?

One of the worst things about the criminal justice system is the inability to make this "right". My penance is to survive a harsh place for more years than I'd previously been alive. I don't have to do anything but survive. How is that worth what they spend on incarceration? But I refuse to simply sit and wait to be released from prison. They have programs, but they are mostly voluntary and are poorly managed by facilitators that are undermined by the governing security mentality that holds us at our worst. We have to actively work to find ways to pay forward.

I got involved in restorative justice early in my bid and believe it is the future of incarceration although it is currently underutilized. In 2016 in Stillwater, I attended a weekend restorative justice retreat called VOCARE (Victims, Offenders, Community, A Restorative Event), which amounted to a 4-day grief counseling group. 4 inmates incarcerated for gun violence related homicides sat with 3 people directly affected by violent crime, with 3 community members and 2 facilitators to share their stories in hopes to foster healing.

Eighteen months prior to the group Char lost her only son Paul to violence. The program was billed as a surrogacy effort. We were standing in for the "offenders" they could not confront in their own situations. We were told we would literally be the "bad guys". This was an opportunity to be of some use. There aren't many chances to be part of a solution from in here. Char and I naturally clicked. The program meant to be one thing, but a different surrogacy happened. Despite the discouragement of the DOC, Char stayed in touch. After some stumbling to define our connection, I now call her my godmother and me her godson – it fit.

I was telling her about you the other day and she said, "oh, I'll have to invite him for coffee." She's at the top of her field with a Ph.D. in child psychology. She has a program that infuses restorative practices in alternative schools. She is such a genuine soul and an important person in my life. I hope it's not too weird or jarring to connect you?

Please take care of yourself. Talk to you soon!
Fausto

5.30.20

Dear Fausto,

Where to start? After my last letter I immediately started another one, but as I was writing I got a text telling me to watch a video from South Minneapolis. You know how the world has been turned upside down since.

Over these last few days I've thought of you so many times. I've wondered what you are feeling/thinking and how these events are affecting the culture at Rush City. I can only imagine the scope of the meaning this has for you, your friends and your family.

I don't know what I'm thinking. I live in South Minneapolis and my studio is in St Paul. Each day I ride my bike past 38th and Chicago where Floyd was killed and down Lake Street past the 3rd precinct. In the morning the mood is somber, like a wake. In the evening it is both celebratory and angry. But I always end up in my safe home or workplace, protected by privilege. I don't believe that my perspective is valuable to you or anyone else. I've thus far declined to cover the event for the publications that have approached me. I don't feel like I have anything to add. I've reached out to a local organization to try and support local Black photographers. I'd rather hear their voices. I'd rather hear your voice.

Speaking of which, I just found your Washington Post article! "The Visiting Room" is fantastic!!!! And, needless to say, these two passages made an impression:

I was sitting across from my girlfriend in the visiting room of the Minnesota Correctional Facility at Stillwater three years into my stay there, nodding in understanding as she vented about her latest drama with co-workers. My gaze drifted over her shoulder and landed on a couple and their kid while they all posed for an inmate photographer. As the small family smiled for the camera, a memory jolted loose: I suddenly remembered being in this same room 20 years ago, as a 6-year-old...

After my girlfriend left, I dug through old photographs in my cell and found one that took my breath away. In it, my sister is clinging to one side of Mom's hip as I rest on the other side. We're all dressed up: I'm wearing a clip-on tie and gray cowboy boots. We took this photo at our apartment before we drove to Stillwater, where my mom married Hermon in the visiting room. My mom was 27 when this photo was taken — about the same age I was while holding the photo in my cell.

Incredible!!! I want to see this picture! The fact that you've learned to do something positive — to create and connect — in the face of everyday brutality is a profound achievement. This is the voice the world needs right now more than anything.

In your last letter you mentioned your depression and the fact that you've recently felt more at peace. You asked if art could help rewire our brains. Whether one is drowning in oppression or depression, having a purpose seems to be the most essential lifeline. I'm not sure how much it matters what that purpose is. It can be writing a novel, knitting a sweater, running a marathon, preaching the gospel, whatever. Focused attention does seem to rewire the brain, yes.

That said, some forms of attention do seem healthier than others. The Guinness Book record holder for eating the most hot dogs in one minute (11) is undoubtedly less healthy than the record holder for the longest continuous run (350 miles over 80 hours without food or sleep). Photography gives me a purpose; a place to focus my attention. But I sometimes question its healthiness. If my purpose were to be a caregiver or educator, for example, I think I would be a healthier person. But do we choose our mission, or does it choose us?

Whatever the case, I'm sure glad you found your purpose. Your honest expression of pain and love has great meaning to me.

Your friend,
Alec

5.31.20

Hey Alec,

Just when you think things can't get any crazier in the world, huh? My thoughts and emotions are so complicated. I keep seeing the word "justice" being thrown around and it's frustrating. For years now I've watched these absurd killings by police from a cell. Then people cry out for "justice" like we even have a grasp on what that means.

What they mean is prison, because that's what we've been trained to believe accountability looks like. Especially in the minority and impoverished communities. The rallies have been based on this idea of imprisoning police and holding them to the same standard that we, as said community, are held to despite our lack of training and resources to succeed in a systematically unequal society.

In the simplest terms they're talking about equality. Like people are mad about cops not going to prison in the same way "criminals" do, which is all coded language that goes back to the Nixon era. We are taught to believe that when you break the law you go to prison. So when people break the law and they don't go to prison, it emphasizes the disparities and builds further frustration magnifying the built-in inequalities. When I was in the suburbs, I didn't have to worry about getting robbed or brutally harassed by police. Drugs are social out there, well at least before the meth and heroin wave hit. When I went to the cities it was a complete culture shift. The threats were on all sides if you were part of a certain demographic. The situations are more complicated than outsiders say and I don't want to speak for everyone, nor do I want to justify violence. Prison is for certain people; it is not the answer, and certainly is not justice. Who goes to prison and who doesn't has exposed the true intentions of the criminal justice system further, adding to all the data we already have that states the now obvious conclusion: it's not about rehabilitation or healing what's broken. It's about politics, condemnation and punishment for a certain demographic. So to see these countless individuals avoid prosecution and conviction time and time again exposes the nature of the system and its core hypocrisy.

Yet I am guilty of what I've done, along with my brothers in here caught up in a violent street/gang/drug culture. We stand accountable and are trying to find ways to be part of the solution.

The constitution and general idea of law abstracts our definition of equality. On that level we are angry because it's "unfair". We have this absurd notion that there is such a thing as "fair" and that this abstraction we call "justice" is universal and should be the answer. But with these blatantly unequal standards we don't get to the point of questioning the value of imprisonment because we can't even get the convictions when people like Philando Castile get murdered by our trained protectors.

To continuously hear people cry out for "justice" is gut-wrenching. There is no equality. I think about the cop in Dallas who recently broke into the wrong apartment and then killed a man — eating ice cream in his own home — and how she received something like an eight-year sentence, of which she'll do a fraction. I think of the Somali cop Noor's conviction for killing the white woman in the alley not too long ago and the sentence he received. So what does justice look like for George Floyd?

Not too long ago, Antionette Johnson sat in the backseat of a car when her boyfriend, unbeknownst to her, went around the corner and killed a guy. They gave her a life sentence as an accomplice because she wouldn't testify against him. A life sentence. She's got small children. And they haven't even arrested those other officers in Floyd's case, and even if and when they do, I'm betting their combined prison sentences won't equal hers as an accomplice. I know tons of guys in similar situations who hold a fraction of culpability compared to trained officers who literally "know better". So the whole idea of justice as equality is absurd to me in the first place, as I sit here rightfully condemned yet disproportionally sentenced.

I also think about the inequality in sentencing. If I were to kill a police officer, I'd receive an automatic 1st-degree murder charge and upon conviction an automatic life sentence without the possibility of parole. In sentencing terms, the value of a police officer's life is more valuable than a citizen's. And although they signed up for the job and have proper training, their supposed heroics entitles them to justifiability even despite a long record of abuses, a license to kill with qualified immunity. Among all of these 'good cops' that supposedly represent the majority, where is the blue line of accountability drawn?

I am an outlaw. Not because I'm a criminal or villain or am seeking to get over on the system. I am an outlaw because I was raised never feeling like the system had my people's best interests in mind. We always kept guns and held our own council. The system was just something that usually confined and limited while mocking our struggles for social mobility. Inequalities are normal and I've never believed in these abstract terms used to control others. And I am well aware that most people have disqualified my opinion or perspective on any of these matters; but maybe this type of voice is the missing piece to solve the puzzle?

Even now, I live within a hypocritical oppression that doesn't want me to evolve into a better person, yet holds me ultra-accountable for the behaviors of all those around me. The Department of Corrections is supposed to be the final stop on the road to justice and on the surface, it is literally responsible for our "correction". I've been in here for 17 years and have had to fight to define redemption for myself. I know that none of this is justice. This system creates more problems and solves nothing. None of this happened in a vacuum. You can't protest in the parking lot of the factory and ignore the pipeline spilling toxicity into the rivers. There are social factors at play, even in Officer Chauvin's callousness, seen clearly in our current President. We are all responsible for these men of American heritage who know no parameters, save the cage they create for others.

Yet I still think about Derek Chauvin with a degree of empathy. I am a murderer, a person who knows the capable depths of the human experience. I stand accountable and own my past and am not afraid of representing a complicated perspective. Chauvin is just as much a product of his environment as I was, or as any young man figuring out his identity within a violent upbringing.

The culture of Rush City is still shitty. This Covid virus still has everything suspended, although word is that the balloon shop is going to open at half capacity this week. I'm currently not working, but it's at the expense of privileges. We're in a "work to play" State, so if I don't have a job then I can only come out of my cell for a couple of hours a day. The guard union adopts the same adversarial mentality that plagues the police departments. To a hammer, everything is a nail. Some of these guards are decent, but a lot of them are Type-A sadists who dominate and steer the oppressive culture. It's the same complicit nature here as with those cops. One asshole does what they want and those with him ride out bad actions based on an ideology of solidarity.

"Do we choose our purpose, or does it choose us?" indeed my friend. A real chicken & egg conundrum. I have another layer of wonder in questioning whether prison was a necessary element of my growth as an artist. I have always inclined towards art, but what if I would have found a mentor like you earlier, who would I have been? And at what expense?

Oh, yeah, so no, you never told me about the beach experience. When I first asked a friend to look up your address, I asked her to send me anything she could print out of yours. She sent me a brief article about your first book about the Mississippi River and something about your epiphany on the beach. It was part of the reason I decided to take a chance and reached out. I dug your perspective about this epiphany and craved an artistic connection, so I took a shot in the dark and decided to write.

I pray you and yours are doing well,
C. Fausto

6.4.20

Dear Fausto,

Since reading your letter I've been pausing every time I hear the word "justice". There's never going to be impartiality in deciding what is morally upright just as there's no such thing as fairness. I've been ruminating on this quote by Cornell West that's almost like a Zen koan: "Never forget that justice is what love looks like in public."

The linking of justice with love doesn't come naturally — most of us intuitively link it to revenge. There's something powerful about connecting it to love instead. Here's another Cornell West quote I came across:

The fundamental question for the wise person is: How do we wounded and scarred creatures choose to be wounded-healers, not wounded-hurters, or scarred-helpers, not scarred-playa-haters? And hope gives us strength to try to have it so — to try to keep struggling for more love, more justice, more freedom, and more democracy.

The best example of linking love and justice is what you wrote about having a degree of empathy for Derek Chauvin. Holy fuck! Even if it is only the tiniest sliver of empathy, the ability to stop and reflect that way is true wisdom.

The other night I went to the first social event I've been to since the pandemic. It was my daughter's boyfriend's graduation party. The only people there were his parents (the first time we met them) and grandparents. It turns out that both of his grandparents were former police sergeants in the Twin Cities. After talking about how horrific George Floyd's death was, both were complaining about how all of the cops under their command lived out in the suburbs (they live in South Minneapolis). I'm not saying these people weren't complicit in our abysmal justice system. I'm sure if I investigated more, I'd find troubling information. But if someone probed me long enough, wouldn't they also find dirt? Aren't I complicit too?

That said, some of us are more evolved than others and there are a lot of assholes in power. There's no bigger asshole than the most powerful one of them all. I'm trying hard not to rant about T***p in my correspondence with you since I obsess over him every day. But his latest calls to "DOMINATE" followed by tear-gassing non-violent protesters so that he could do a photo-op with a Bible — it's beyond the beyond. I'm struggling to muster a shred of empathy.

I'm still trying to figure out what the recent events mean for me as a photographer. I've had several magazine requests to photograph the protests, but I've turned them all down. Today for the first time I referred a publication to a list of Black photographers working in Minneapolis. I've never done such a thing or, honestly, thought to have done such a thing before. So, baby steps.

During this morning's bike ride down Chicago and Lake Street, I reflected on the subject of time. For vast stretches of my life, time made sense. Seconds, minutes, days, months, years. But the combination of Twitter, 2020, and the fact that my children are teenagers has shattered my understanding of time. One day feels like a week, the next goes by in a minute. This phenomenon is problematic for me as a photographer. My job is to stop time and ideally make an image that stands the test of its passing. What does that even mean any more?

Reflecting on this question, I thought of an iconic photograph made by a photographer named Josef Koudelka in 1968. It's of a man's wristwatch at the beginning of the Soviet invasion of Prague. "I do not remember them nor they me," Koudelka said forty years later, "You cannot rely on your memories — but you can rely on your pictures."

With this in mind, on today's daily visit to the George Floyd memorial site, I made this picture on my iPhone:

When I returned to my studio, I read an interview with Koudelka from 2018 in which he's asked, "So what matters, Josef?" This was his answer:

Everything. Everything matters. Everything. Every day is a gift… This morning, it mattered very much that the sun came out at 8:18 am. Tomorrow it is going to matter very much, if I am here, that the sun is going to rise at 8:16 am. Everything matters. I don't take things for granted. Everything is present for me. And if something beautiful happens, I try to enjoy and appreciate it as much as possible. You know, we are all different. At the same time, we are all very much the same.

And each of us is trying to find the way to be in this world, and there is no one way.

This appreciation of each moment leads me to the subject of meditation. You asked me about Helsinki. This relates to what I've written to you before about being a connoisseur of distance.

I've always seen myself as photographing the space between myself and my subject:

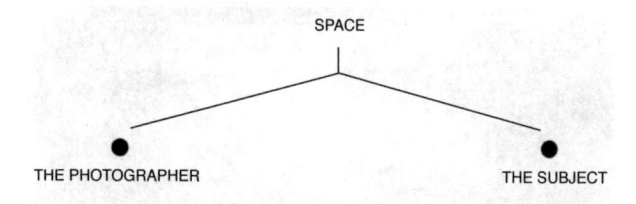

```
                    SPACE
                      |
            ┌─────────┴─────────┐
            ●                   ●
      THE PHOTOGRAPHER      THE SUBJECT
```

In the fall of 2016, I had an exhibition in Finland. On the plane, I did a bunch of meditating. It seemed to have a more substantial effect because of the altitude. When I arrived in Helsinki, I was full of energy, so I went for a walk. I visited a beautiful wooden building called Kampii Chapel, "The Chapel of Silence". It has no religious affiliation. It's just a place to be quiet in the heart of the city. After that, I went for a long walk to a little island. The sun was starting to go down and I meditated by the water. I had what I can only describe as an awakening. It was utterly unlike anything I've ever experienced in my life. I'm sure various factors were at play. I was jetlagged; I'd had a lot of fresh air, etc. But it didn't matter. The entire world felt different. While walking back to my hotel, I felt connected to everything. I felt incredible love for every single person I saw on the street.

The next day I had to give a lecture on my photography. But I felt so transformed that I stayed up all night rewriting everything. I showed the diagram above and then questioned publicly how I would respond as an artist now that the space between me and the world had collapsed like this:

Things changed dramatically after that. It's a long story to explain what I did next, and this is already turning into a novel, so I'll just say that I didn't make a lot of work for the next year. Mostly I meditated. It was the happiest year of my life. But after a year of this, I realized that I needed to get back to work. At first it felt amazing, particularly when I photographed people. There was still space between myself and the subject, but I had an awareness that something else was at play. I started to think that maybe I wasn't just photographing space, but also energy:

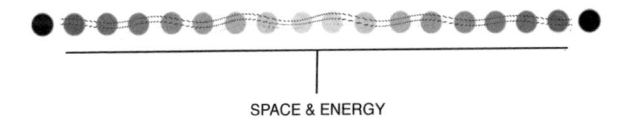

SPACE & ENERGY

What's both interesting and problematic for me is that I learned I need that space and energy to produce strong work. If I meditate all of the time and reach a state of equilibrium, my work becomes so understated that it only speaks to other people who are in a similar state of mind. It's like minimalist music. In the end, my work is more successful when I dig deep into my vulnerabilities — when I speak from my wounded and scarred energy. I'd like to make joyful pictures, but for whatever reason that is a rarity for me. My energy has a lot of darkness.

This brings me back to your question about whether art can rewire our brains. Absolutely. Art has allowed me to work with my darkness in a way that isn't too destructive. Does it do good? Maybe it gives a small amount of comfort to others experiencing darkness, but I'm not sure that's enough. So hopefully I can do good in other ways. I'm not a great teacher, but I'm trying to learn how I can be helpful in different ways.

One of the things I've been thinking a lot about is your dual contribution as a creative writer and as a prison-rights activist. Writing a poem can be healing to both you and the person reading it, but it sounds like a different kind of healing than what happens in the restorative justice program you described. Doing both of those things is a way to make yourself better and the world better.

I've yammered on for too long. I'm sorry I haven't reached out to your Aunt yet. This last week has been so overwhelming.

Your friend,
Alec

6.18.20

Hey Alec,

It's funny you say your obsessed with Trump and how you won't even spell his name! Haha, I'm definitely in agreement, although because of my outlaw nature I view it more comically, I suppose. I get madder at those who follow him or justify his bullshit. Yet he is what America has manifest; a trumped-up caricature of most. This exposed system is finally under indictment. In my 17 years of incarceration, I've never watched as much news as I have this month. It's oddly the first time I've felt this much hope in America.

I imagine society is entering a mourning phase confronting the fact that things will never be the same. First the pandemic, then the deconstruction of how we've always viewed the criminal justice system and the systemic racism embedded in everything. There is a very real correlation between losing someone and entering a new paradigm while processing through grief stages. It took me at least five years to even begin to grasp the reality of my imprisonment. You get the "rules" have changed. Physically you adapt. For me it would manifest in lack: sex, concrete money, phones, physical touch, visits — watching loved ones disappear through the doors, then getting used to strip search after every visit, standing in line for a 15-minute phone call. Shit, even ten years in I'd still feel the vibration of my cell phone going off in my pocket like a phantom limb I lost.

Emotionally, I've never really adjusted in any healthy sense, save what we talked about with art & purpose. In here, I see it calcify in anger and defensiveness unaddressed.

Most men assume the role as a victim of the DOC and neglect even to acknowledge their behavior or victims. The system isn't developed to help victims heal or convicts rehabilitate. Most guys don't even address the shift and just begin a stasis of waiting to get out – daydreamers escaping reality. I can't even remember who I was out in the world pre-incarceration. I reached a point where I literally had to put my old life to death and figure out how to move forward into this new normal. Japanese Samurai live life as if they are already dead, completely devoted to a charge. When I took a life, I sacrificed my own without understanding the terms. Now I must find a way to create, in order to combat the destruction.

It's easy for me to look forward to a new future because life has always felt harsh for me. But I'm curious to know how people feel about the shift from a successful perspective. The "system" has worked for a hell of a lot of people and it seems like that is the root of a lot of the resistance to change.

Where do you see yourself in all of this? It was interesting to hear what you said about your daughter's boyfriend's grandparents and your interaction with them. I believe societal progress is more dependent on these types of conversations. I do not believe that people are maliciously racist or even aware of the root of their anger or distrust. There's been a lot of talk about unconscious bias. When we were in the writing workshops critiquing other people's work, one of the first things we learned was to be aware of our personal bias. Most of our initial reactions to things are underlying emotional connections to events from our past we had little control over and are largely left unexamined. At first it was hard not to personalize our responses. Idk Alec – I think it all boils down to the simplicity of communication. We don't know how to give or take criticisms, and we get so offended when people disagree, which results in polarization. There is a lack of empathy in all of us. My pain and hardships don't entitle me to anything, but I hope to at least be heard. We are entering a time of greatness – where we can examine our cages and confront that our parameters can be limitless when we connect with "others".

I think about those photos of lynch mobs that used to be postcards (Eula Bliss had a great essay about telephone poles and lynching in *Notes From No Man's Land*) – the faces of those posing for the pic. But I also think about those on the fringe of the photo, outside the shot: those men's family & friends, the community, those passing those horrific scenes – the complicit. But now no one can say they never saw a lynching. And we have witnessed an event that literally can define our character regardless of who we are and what community we belong to or the culture we claim. We can all be Americans finally.

The evolutions of your awareness or understanding of that space between you and your subjects is so universal. I see so many people who are oblivious to the very existence of such space. It's the root of communication issues. For there to be any success, there's gotta be an agreement about the space between. I see so many people talking at and past each other, unable to grasp or connect with that energized space that holds so much possibility. Is it simply a lack of empathy? Or a lack of awareness?

There is a writing prompt I used in Stillwater with a mental health writing group I facilitated. We'd write about random snapshots for five minutes, then pass the pictures to the left. It was always fascinating to hear people's unconscious biases emerge in the diversity of approaches to the same subjects. There was this one that sticks out in my memory of a 50s era family at a kitchen table. The mother was finishing cooking with a certain look on her face while the father was obviously admonishing the son while pushing food around his plate. It was the only photo that never had a variety of interpretations. The staging was so specific that it left little room for creativity. I thought of something my High School basketball coach still tells me: "Say things in a way not to be misunderstood." But it also challenged me to push the boundaries and find distinction, like writing from the point of view of the oven or by including a person outside of the frame. What can I add to the conversation that hasn't been discussed?

Thanks for sharing your Helsinki story. I thought about Ralph Waldo Emerson's essay "Nature", or was it "The Poet"? One of the few good things at Rush City is that there is a small courtyard attached to the unit. Just a small fenced-in area with four tables, a pull-up bar, and a cornhole table. In Stillwater our yard was boxed in with huge walls. Rush City has a few layers of fence surrounded by dense forests — but there is a stronger sense of nature. After my second year here, I read Emerson's essay and connected with his description of nature as our source and inspiration. The beauty of the sky up here had me in awe at times. Such a vast haven of vibrant color and light. Just the thought of you on that beach, with all of those factors lining up to energize that specific moment is inspiring. And maybe even a little ironic in the sense that you are one to capture moments in time, but you had an experience no lens could ever do justice to.

There are so many layers and angles to this. That's what I love about my people: artists. Purpose, impactful potential, process, collaboration, craft! It's a beautifully multifaceted life, isn't it — I'm happy to be living in this time. So full of pain & suffering, yet so invigorated by hope & faith. I hope you are doing well, my friend, and are surrounded by love. These are beautifully uncomfortable times and I fully believe that we are up to the challenges ahead. Talk to you soon.

Best Regards,
Fausto

6.29.20

Dear Chris,

Having now met several people that call you by that name, I wonder if I can too? But, for the record, I think Fausto is one of the all-time great pen names.

2020 is the most screwed up year in my lifetime, but I'll always treasure the fact that it's allowed me to do a deep dive into the Chris/Fausto universe. And, man, does it keep expanding. I mean, Char: what an incredible woman! It's incredible to meet someone who has faced – is facing – so many of life's biggest challenges with such grace.

Char's optimism prompted me to discuss the broader issue of happiness with her. Many years ago, I read a book called "The Geography of Bliss". The author traveled to some of the world's happiest countries (Switzerland, Iceland, Qatar, Bhutan) to see how different populations define and pursue happiness. The primary way that researchers study happiness is by simply asking people to attach a subjective number for their happiness between 1 (the least happy) and 10. In a place like Switzerland, people on average give the number 8 whereas in a country like Moldova it is 5. I became fascinated by this subject and would often ask people I meet about their number. Char, facing everything she's facing – the death of a child, divorce, cancer – told me she was an 8.

I've given a lot of thought about my own happiness number. For a year I even tracked it. When I averaged things out, I was approximately a 7. But that was following my year of meditation, so I was still riding high. I think my default is around 6. I don't know if it's nature or nurture, but at a certain point in childhood or adolescence, I think we set our baseline. Health, freedom, and stability can cause that number to rise and fall, but a large part of our relative happiness seems baked in.

It's so wonderful meeting someone with such a positive outlook like Char. But I can also find value in meeting people with low numbers. It's like the difference between reggae music and the blues; both can comfort. This reminds me of a quote I came across yesterday in the wake of the death of the designer Milton Glaser. He said:

The important thing I can tell you is that there is a test to determine whether someone is toxic or nourishing in your relationship to them. Here is the test: You have spent some time with this person, either you have a drink or go for dinner or you go to a ball game. It doesn't matter very much but at the end of that time you observe whether you are more energized or less energized. Whether you are tired or whether you are exhilarated. If you are more tired then you have been poisoned. If you have more energy you have been nourished. The test is almost infallible and I suggest you use it for the rest of your life.

My meeting with Char was nourishing, as has been this exchange with you. It makes sense that you both connected.

After meeting Char I was eager to get out and see your Aunt Kathy, especially since I was going to be leaving town. The day before my flight I made the drive out to Isanti. She was able to find an envelope of snapshots for me to look at, but unfortunately most of their photographs are in deep storage.

It was fascinating to see the photos of you as you transformed from a little boy to a teenager. But for our conversation, I was struggling to figure out how to use them.

Perhaps I was looking more for the aura of your life rather than the specificity of your appearance. My favorite picture was of you as a little boy, presumably waiting for the bus on the first day of school.

My attraction to this photo is mostly the lack of detail. Your face is obscured in shadows and the entire top of the picture is washed in light. While there's a sentimental "Wonder Years" like quality to it that is enhanced by the suburban cul-de-sac, there's something particularly mournful about this picture. You know how I respond to the feeling of distance — that's a part of it. But there's something else. When I look at this picture, the first thing I always see is a short, balding man waving to an empty road. Intellectually I know it is a boy waving to his mom, but my brain inverts the image.

There's a way in which the absence of people, or just the suggestion of them, allows the viewer inside the image.

Looking at this picture, I can enter the photo as any number of characters: the boy, the mother, or the bald little man.

What does this have to do with you and your childhood? Not so much. But I am fascinated by that cul-de-sac. The yard looks so big. Do you remember where it was? Who lived across the street? Other memories from that time? One of the things I noted about the other snapshots was how white everybody was except for you. There's a photo of a birthday party with a gaggle of white women and a graduation event in which you are flocked by young white men. I'm wondering how it felt to grow up in what looks to be a largely white world.

The more I looked at the snapshots of you, the more I became interested in the backgrounds. As an experiment, I cropped them so that there was just a fragment of you in the frame. This helped me walk around a bit more in your world. I'm wondering if these images trigger any memories or associations for you.

Do you often think about your teenage bedroom? Is it connected in any way to the experience of having a cell? In both cases, these rooms technically belong to someone else and exist under their rules, but it's a place to at least try and carve out your own identity.

Speaking of solitary rooms, I should tell you about the room I'm writing to you from. I'm currently in Rome doing a job for Gucci. I had to come here two weeks before my assignment to quarantine. I didn't know in advance what quarantine would require. When I arrived, things looked quite similar to home, with restaurants open, etc. But on my second day I got a call from the health department checking to make sure I wasn't leaving the hotel. They

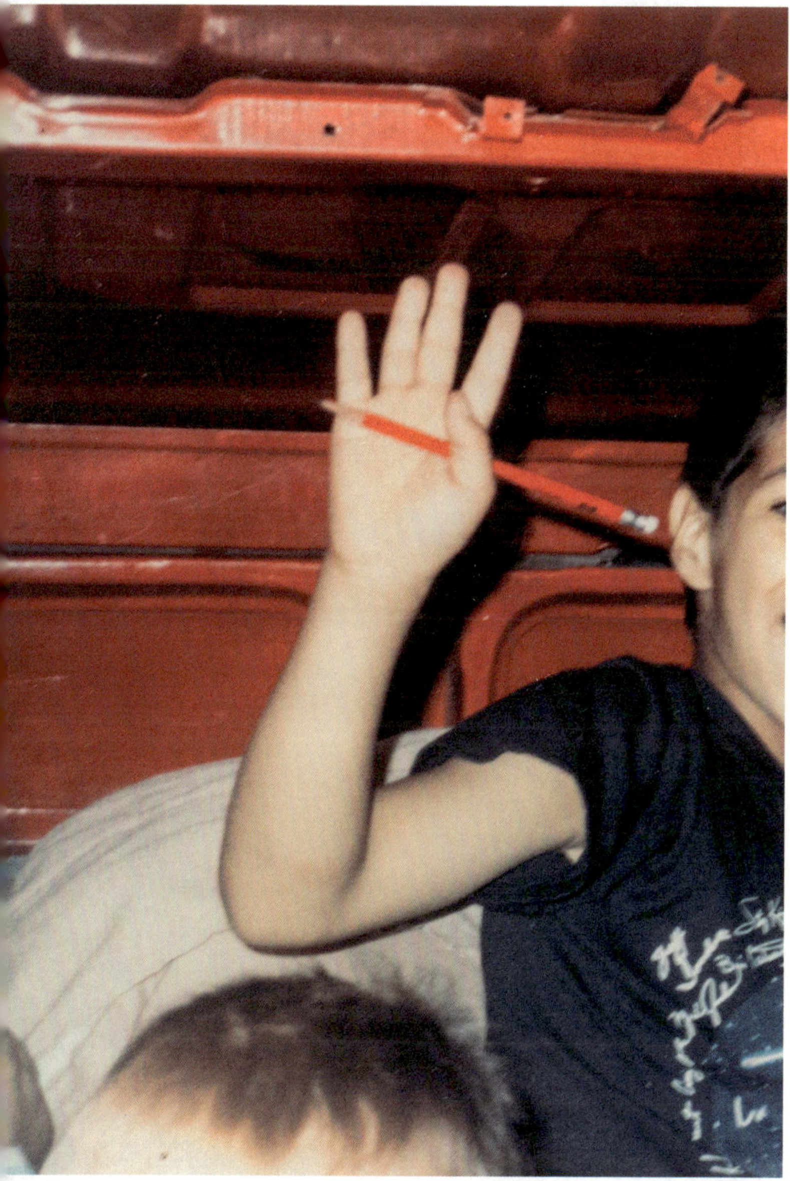

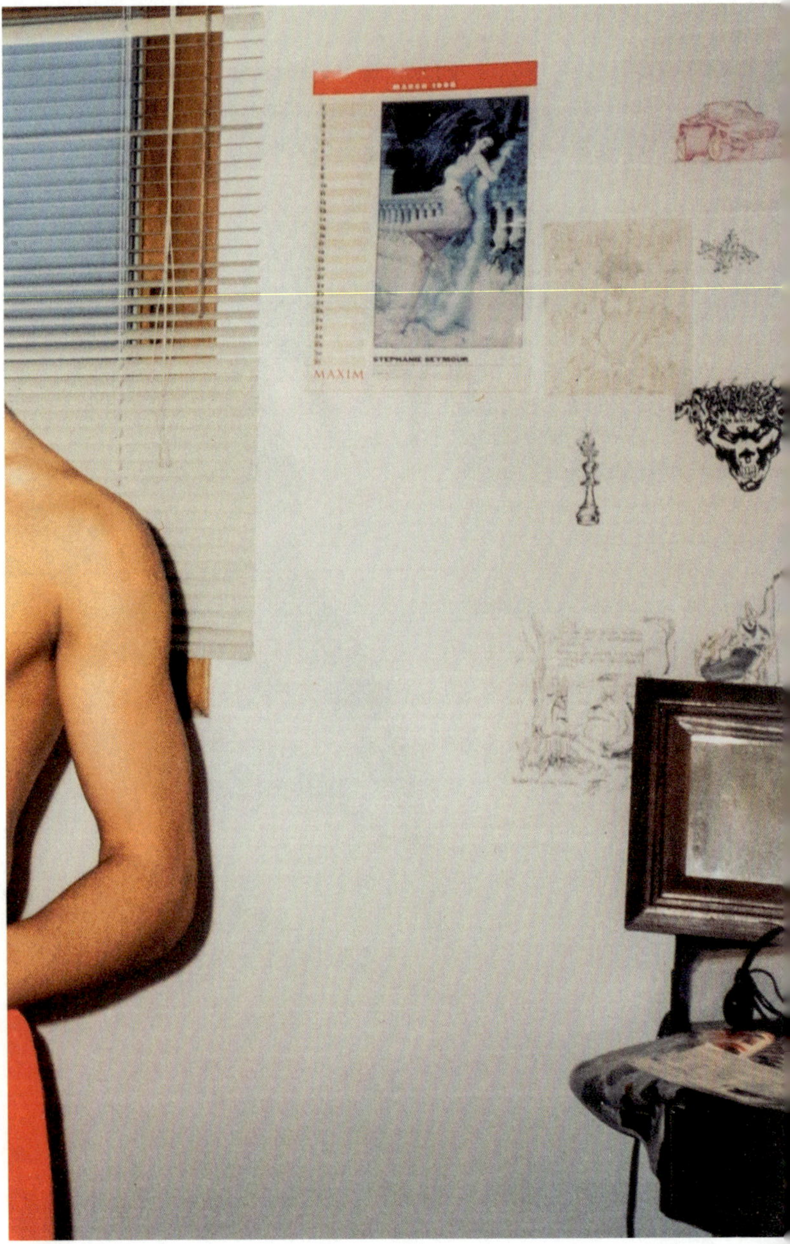
STEPHANIE SEYMOUR
MAXIM

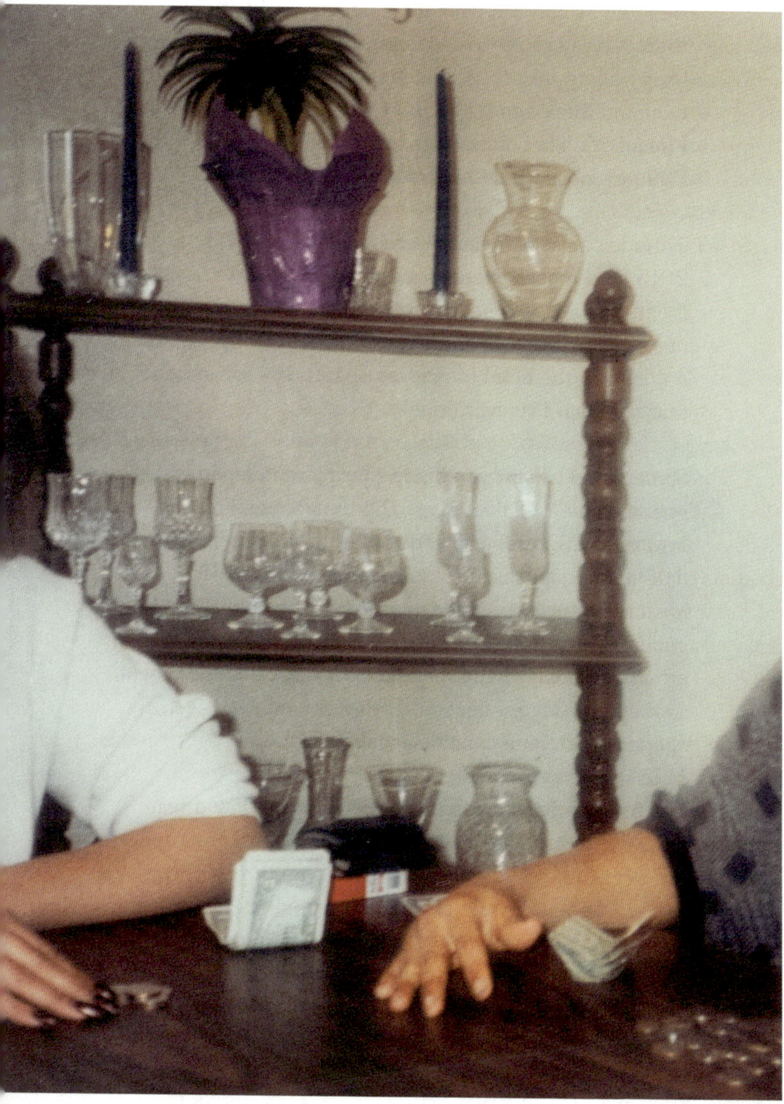

said they would call back the next day. So I felt obligated to stay in my room. The embarrassing truth is that I was happy about this. I was grateful to have time to sit and read and think and write. But I feel shitty telling you this. I mean, it's like I'm in the most luxurious prison cell ever. Pablo Escobar would be jealous.

This idea of isolating myself like this is not new to me. In 2015 I did an assignment for the *New York Times*. I pitched them the idea of going to a luxurious hotel in Tokyo (the one where the movie *Lost in Translation* was filmed) and not leaving the hotel for the entire trip. It was the best magazine job I've ever done.

Something I've always wanted to explore in Japan is the phenomenon of Hikikomori. The term means "pulling inward, being confined" and is used for the approximately half-million Japanese people who don't leave their rooms. Most often these are male adolescents, though now it has gone on for so long that many of them are older. They are afraid of the world and they have mothers that feed them, so they just stay in their rooms and live online. I feel connected to these people.

My first few days here were indeed spent online. I fear there's a decent chance I could turn into Hikikomori! Over the weekend, the *Star Tribune* opened up their archives for free. I went down a research rabbit hole. The subject I was particularly interested in was the killing of a cop at the Pizza Shack restaurant on Lake Street in 1992. In the aftermath of George Floyd, I brought this up with several people, but they were mostly younger and had forgotten it.

I was 22 when the Pizza Shack murder happened. I was away at college, but I knew Lake Street well. At that time my family lived near Uptown and my girlfriend (now wife) lived just over the Lake Street bridge in St Paul. Driving Lake Street was a romantic ritual back then. Now it is a work ritual. For the last fourteen years I've lived in South Minneapolis and my studio is in the Midway area of St Paul. I wonder how many thousands of times I've driven the length of Lake Street. I was always fascinated by the cultural variety: the punks and yuppies of Uptown, the Mexican and Somali bodegas and restaurants, the streetwalkers and drug dealers, and then, crossing over into St Paul, the return to wealth and security. I always knew that I came from the white, privileged bookends of Lake Street, but I never really digested what this meant until George Floyd's murder. A couple of days after I crossed the bridge onto Marshal and stared in awe as women golfed while just down the road Lake Street burned. This new outlook on myself and my city is why I wanted to return to the news coverage of the Pizza Shack murder.

What I'd forgotten about the murder was the police brutality incident that prompted it. The day before the policeman was murdered by the Vice Lords gang, a blind and disabled black man was pushed off a bus and beaten by transit police for being a dime short on bus fare. Obviously, this doesn't justify the murder, but it got me interested in the blind black man. His name was LeRoy Gray. Six months after the Pizza Shack murder, I read that he pleaded guilty to not paying the bus fare. All the newspaper says about him is that he was "presented as a victim" at some protests. It's galling. This was only a year or so after Rodney King and Gray was blind and disabled. But now LeRoy Gray isn't even a footnote to this history.

I did more digging on him and found two more stories on LeRoy Gray. There was one from 1964 with a graphic picture of him on a stretcher after the shooting that had blinded him. The other story from 1975 was about a car crash he was in that killed his brother. It's hard for me to imagine a life full of such hardship that it makes the newspaper three separate times but ends up being totally forgotten.

I just started reading *Invisible Man* by Ralph Ellison. There's a scene where a white man bumps into the unnamed main character and then insults him. When the white man refuses to apologize, the main character beats him. He writes:

I can hear you say, "What a horrible, irresponsible bastard!" And you're right. I leap to agree with you... But to whom can I be responsible, and why should I be, when you refuse to see me... Responsibility rests upon recognition, and recognition is a form of agreement... And if he had yelled for a policeman, wouldn't I have been taken for the offending one?

LeRoy Gray seems like he was one of the countless invisible people. We now try to remember some of their names, but it's like memorizing all of the names on the headstones of a cemetery.

Sorry for the ramble. I don't know what will come of any of this, but I know it will be something meaningful. I hope you feel the same way.

With gratitude and friendship,
Alec

7.6.20

Hey Alec,

Of course you can call me Chris. It's funny to think of Fausto catching on; it's my father's name. I used to think it was too different. I'm not going to hold on too tightly to a name shift. If it occurs naturally, I'm all for it, but I do love it as a pen name.

I know, right?! How great is Char? I am not surprised her happiness number is 8. I agree with you about a "baseline". Throughout the years of analysis, I certainly believe there are genetics to mood. It took me a long time to realize that my depression was a mood disorder and not an aspect of my personality. But I also wonder about the other factors at play. In the show *Madmen* there was a quote that stuck to my ribs about dissatisfaction being a symptom of ambition. It makes me wonder if happiness is a goal, or can I only hope for moments of contentment in between challenges. That's what I love about the potency of poems.

That poison Milton Glaser talks about is so real. In here it is especially tangible. It begins with the personnel, the attitudes and actions of the guards that clearly dictate the environment that makes already broken people worse. Can you imagine a drug rehabilitation facility that antagonizes its patients & perpetually treats them as the worst versions of themselves?

But it isn't limited to authorities. We all experience these broken people that pollute the environment at work or in social capacities. We have friends and relationships we've hung onto out of a sense of familiarity. But what to do about it? When we see toxic perspectives crying out, do we step up and challenge them in domestic settings? Do we find a way to ensure that love Cornell West spoke of – do we take hold of our personal responsibility to be the change we desire? Like how you recommended Black photographers?

I love that quote because it speaks to the need to maintain a balance that can create an ebb and flow of that energy. I think of Char and how much she dictates her environment by simply bringing her energy into the room. It's what I hope to be as an artist, a conduit of those energies that can reinvent the narrative. It reminds me of how you talk about your work speaking to the state of disassociation and loneliness. How you'd figured out how to harness such an internal feeling, convert that energy and put it out into the world to serve as the comfort to remind me and so many others that we're not alone. For me, those types of works are instrumental to my artistic development and just as important as any physical health treatment. Art, in its many abundantly vast forms, is a medicine for the soul. Before I go into the photos, I read a poem by Robert Hayden that reminded me of you: "The Diver." Here are the opening lines:

Sank through easeful
azure. Flower
creatures flashed and
shimmered there-
lost images
fadingly remembered.

That house in that first picture, 8907 7th St in Blaine, was the closest thing I know of a childhood home. Kathy and Steve were in the process of buying it, making them the very first homeowners in the family, all migrated from the projects of Rockford and Joliet, Illinois. Much like many families climbing the social mobility ladder, they never hesitated to carry us on their backs; be it out of a sense of obligation, a kind heart or the combination, they became the hub and that house was the base. My mother, sister, me and my lil' brother spent most of our days in section-8 apartment complexes but in between buildings we certainly stayed with them for a significant amount of time in that house.

Across the street, where the sun creates that silhouette between the houses is a huge retaining wall separating the neighborhood from the K-Mart parking lot. It was at that K-Mart around the age of ten where I discovered my invisibility flipped a switch with security guards. Accused of stealing a cassette tape I put back on the shelf, the guy didn't spare me of the shame by dragging me through the store to prove I put it back. When my sister told my Mom what happened, she called up K-Mart and berated them for their treatment and threatened them with everything she could think of for their racism. It was the first time I'd ever heard my Mom defend me like that and the first time I can remember her confronting the difference between me and the outside world.

I was definitely raised in a white world, the residual effect of my mother's intent to keep us in the suburbs to attend better schools. My identity confusion was further compounded by the absence of my father who was Afro-Cuban and the only one in his family to defect from the island. My mom's brothers, of Lithuanian Jew, Swedish and Irish descent, always told me I wasn't black, that I was Cuban, like that made a difference in how the world at large perceived me. To them it was more about trying to deter me from embracing a street culture they perceived was coming from the rap music I was listening to. When my mom died, I was disconnected from any semblance of Cuban culture without much Spanish and the adverse factors compiling pushing me to retreat within myself.

Looking at the picture of my bedroom wall, I think about how, for some, it's art that saves them. Something like a tree limb extended they grasp and use to reach the riverbank. For me, art was always there but never a sustainable enough thought to keep me from the approaching rapids. It still makes me wonder if it's too late.

I see the drawings hanging on my high school bedroom wall and don't feel so far away, like the art itself opens a timeless portal. The iconography is haunting. A thread pulls all the way back to my 7-yr old self visiting my stepdad in Stillwater Prison. He sent me an ink skull drawn in delicate pen similar to the one on the wall, similar to the hundred or so I've drawn through my incarceration. The gun held by a skeletal hand, the chess piece, the sports car; all a mirror of the symbols I've gravitated to in tattoo designs and art. Even down to the calendar page of a sexualized woman, back arched, leaning seductively with the same allure I still depend on in my depravity. It's almost like I was preparing for prison. Or maybe these decades of pause have arrested my development? My cell, very much a continuation of the bedroom that held my identity reflected back from walls not my own.

But I was never without support. Family poker games [Picture #4] were the ritual at the hub of our family camaraderie. Growing up, it was the reason we collected our spare change, second only to the laundromat. My Mom would always have rolls of quarters wrapped in paper prepared for the games structured around paydays. In all of the years I can't recall one fight over those card games. All the adults would gather around the kitchen table at the house on 7th street to play dealer's choice. These nights were the highlight of my young life. Through the cigarette smoke, laughs, and empty cans, I was designated as waiter earning tips swapping out soda and serving nachos. I'd linger around the table seeking a lap to get a closer view learning all the different games: In-between, Bingo, High card, Low card, Pass card and Black Widow – my mom's favorite. Sometimes someone would come with a completely original game to test out. This was all well before the Texas Hold'em craze. I could always tell when the hand got serious because everyone would stand and lean into the game. We were still a family who depended on every dollar, so the tones and tensions became easy to read. If Mom won, it would dictate how the week would go. There were days I tried to stay up with them but would tap out and wake to only a few people left at the table, my mom always being among them.

Family rules stated we couldn't play until we were fifteen and had our own money to lose. Having lost Mom when I was twelve, I never got the chance to sit across from her, never got to win her money or lose mine to her. Since I've been incarcerated, this family ritual has fallen by the wayside along with most holidays. Traditions from your childhood always seem to change as families expand and grow apart. But I can never forget how it felt those nights. Some guys daydream about a place from in here, but lately I've been thinking about re-establishing some of these rituals from my past that were based on enjoying my people. As I contemplate the future, I envision hosting my own card games bringing together my newly formed family and establishing the camaraderie I remember as a kid.

I hope you are at peace, my friend, and that Rome is treating you well. Peace & Blessings!

Fausto

7.13.20

Dear Chris,

So during my time in quarantine in Rome, I experimented with the idea of making a stand-alone edit of our conversation. After taking our unedited correspondence of 45,000 words and paring it down to 17,000, I felt like something emerged that could be meaningful for others. I sent it to my publisher Michael Mack and he said that he would like to make a small book of our conversation. Michael and I both agree that it should be published quite soon. If you are agreeable, we could give all of the proceeds to charity. Let me know what you think.

Alec

7.16.20

Hey Alec,

There has been a manifestation of that saying, "it's always darkest before the dawn" attached to good news for me in here. Through another series of frustratingly petty events, I wasn't able to reach the kiosk for a couple of days. When I finally did, I saw that your message had been sitting in the inbox for two days! Ugh, but man, how exciting!

The only charity I can definitely distinguish is the Minnesota Prison Writing Workshop (MPWW) because they trained me as a writer and are doing great and important work, so at least a percentage. I'm over the moon! I know that there is work to be done, but am still looking forward to "nerding out" and talking craft when there is time :-)

Be well, my friend! Talk to you soon…

Fausto

7.20.20

Hi Chris,

I'm currently at the airport in Rome. To be honest, the fashion job I did here was kind of idiotic, but I'm grateful that it paid for those two weeks in the hotel to edit our exchange. Sorry about the recent petty shit you've had to endure. Let me know if there's anything you need.

Talk soon, my friend,
Alec

7.27.20

Hey Alec,

The high-end fashion world of Gucci and all those other brands is sort of a conundrum to me. Especially in how much people are willing to pay for a status symbol without having a firm personal foundation established. Yeah, right, thanks Gucci for funding the edits:-)

There's a liberation to writing now that the tone is back to being more conversational and more informal, in my mind anyway. I think I got into a different headspace when I wrote about those snapshots, like I was trying to envision how they'd read to an audience with your other project. It just seems a bit more personal. Now that you've met my people, I am a lot more relaxed and I'm not overthinking about "audience", which is odd right because it's like filming a documentary you want to "act natural", but there's a camera following you. I guess I'm just saying that projects and art aside, being able to talk to you about art and life has helped me through these weary days. It's been a tough couple of years here at Rush City and there doesn't feel like an end, but I can escape through this portal of art and writing and connecting with you and processing thoughts that might not have otherwise been captured. I don't talk to anyone about how dark it gets to anyone any more. Mainly because I know it'll just create a burden for them to carry that they can't do anything about.

I love this Hikikomori concept. I think about getting out and being a parole agent's dream because wherever I end up, I'll be catching up on the shit that I missed. I'll be binge-watching shows and getting lost on the internet. Everyone says that's how you date now anyway. I try not to think about it too much, but lately I've felt a lot closer to the world. Writing has opened my eyes. Maybe it's all the protests and cries for social justice reform. I'm ready to claim a seat at the table. A couple of my Brothers who were with me in the beginning are getting out now. My homie Brickhead just got out early on the Covid release.

That's a trip about LeRoy Gray! To think about all those stories that get glossed over, especially back then, even in the 90s, which shouldn't seem so far away, but shit, I see footage and it looks so retro. All those stories, pre-Internet, just get buried and are reduced to headlines. LeRoy lived a harsh life, invisible for sure.

I struggle with that invisibility concept personally. I feel like I have a responsibility to tell my story and write and work to represent the disenfranchised, but I dream of the day when I can be a producer behind the curtain. The spotlight, too much attention, compliments; all make me internally uncomfortable, but flattered at the same time. So professionally, I think I'm with you in that outsider mentality where there's a buffer. The work is the purpose.

So I'm feeling like it's time to thank you verbally, at least!? Right? My schedule for 'flag' (our hour out) this week is: Tuesday 12:30ish, Wednesday 9am, Thursday 9:20 & 12:30 (we get 2 hours out when we don't have gym or yard) Friday 7:10am-9:10, Saturday 2:30, Sunday 5:15ish. Uggh… let me know if you are available for a 15-minute phone call during these times.

Be well my friend…

7.28.20

Hi Chris,

Yes, let's talk on the phone. Let's shoot for Thursday. Either 9:20 or 12:30, whichever suits you.

I just got back from driving to Wisconsin for a Covid test (for upcoming assignment – I'm sure I don't have it). On the drive, I listened to an interview with André 3000 from OutKast. He has that "outsider mentality" you talked about in your last letter. I like what he said about missing the freedom he had when nobody cared about his music:

I liken it to, if you're a kid, and you're in your room, and you're playing with toys. You have this world going on. The moment when your mom opens the door and says, "André," that world stops. Once the attention is on that world, the world goes away. So, you got to find a way to get back to that place to where you can build those worlds again and not have the eyes, or the judging. That's hard for me, it's really hard for me.

I was surprised by his discomfort with attention, particularly given his flamboyant style, which he also talked about in the interview. When André was young and started growing dreadlocks, he said he needed to cover them up until they grew out. Not wanting to copy Tupac's bandana, he bought a turban at a beauty store. It became his signature style and was a million times cooler than someone just slapping on an expensive brand as a status symbol.

Since we've never met, I better put this on the record now: I have awful style. Hipsters call it "normcore", haha, but to me it's just a way of fading into the background. Along with wearing bland clothes, I have a beard and usually wear a baseball hat. If I could choose a superpower, it would be invisibility.

Speaking of which, I finally finished *Invisible Man*. It's crazy that I didn't know in advance one of the most significant plot points. At the narrative apex, a cop kills an unarmed black man, which leads to rioting and looting. It's during this chaos that the main character falls through an empty manhole and decides to start living life underground.

It's a bleak book, but there's an epilogue that articulates an honest path forward. Ellison's writing here reminded me so much of you:

I condemn and affirm, say no and say yes, say yes and say no. I denounce because though implicated and partially responsible, I have been hurt to the point of abysmal pain, hurt to the point of invisibility. And I defend because in spite of all I find that I love. In order to get some of it down I have to love. I sell you no phony forgiveness, I'm a desperate man —but too much of your life will be lost, its meaning lost, unless you approach it as much through love as through hate. So I approach it through division. So I denounce and I defend and I hate and I love.

Thanks for sharing your condemnations and affirmations with me.

With love and friendship,
Alec

7.31.20

Hey Alec,

It was great to finally hear your voice and weird to think about the layers of introduction we'll go through culminating with meeting face to face. For as socially awkward as I feel and how you described your introverted nature, you have a great sense of humor and there was a calming fluidity to our conversation. I was looking forward to calling back, but we went on lockdown because there were a couple of positive Covid tests in the kitchen unit.

Invisibility has been on my mind ever since you referenced Ellison. If it wasn't enough for me to grow up as an outsider racially and economically, I had to further disenfranchise myself by becoming a felon. Talk about being my own worst enemy. A while back, the Education Director here in Rush City told me in passing that I'd won some award and I'd be interviewed for a poem I wrote called "Seen". I was flattered but I'd never written a poem under that title. With all I had done he didn't even know his own programs or seemed to care enough to get the information right. Emily Baxter founded "We Are All Criminals.org" and had a new photography project called "Seen", showcasing inmates in their natural environments as artists. The weekend before she was scheduled to photograph me, a notoriously antagonistic guard got punched up in the chowhall for pushing a guy over the edge. Since the guard union was in the process of renegotiating a new contract, they used it as a political play and locked the whole facility down. I was surprised when they allowed me to shower after four days then escorted me to the education wing. I was the only inmate out of their cage and could feel disgust in the eyes of guards – reminding I didn't belong among them.

Shortly into the photoshoot, Emily lowered the camera and asked if I was all right. She said I do fine socially, but when I confront the camera a sadness emerges. It took me by surprise and my automatic response was of someone caught in a lie. I stuttered, looking down at the ground for an answer. I felt my eyes welling up and it took everything in me not to break down into sobbing tears. The lens was magic; it either picked up on everything coming through the aperture or emitted an energy to expose me. Am I all right? A question I deflect on the phone and in visiting because I'm never in a safe enough environment to be vulnerable; a question I usually meet with sarcasm and anger among my incarcerated peers. IS anyone alright while in here? Emily was instantly added to a list of people who sincerely cared but could do little more to help me out of this problem I created. So why transfer the burden?

Alec, I'm sure you know all too well that invisible people react to being seen in different ways. I'm curious to hear about your experience with subjects who tense up or act adversely to that space between you, them & the audience represented by the camera. Or is it that most are anxious enough to be seen? Do you coax a shot out that you know looms just under the surface? Emily was well aware of more than I could bear to say, which made me wonder about the common intuition photographers develop behind the lens.

Every time the Education Director came into the room, the energy shifted, and I felt more invisible. Emily asked if we could go into the adjacent main hallway to diversify the background. It was unavoidable that guards would emerge into the background. I could only imagine what they must be thinking as they approached but their actions told me enough.

Emily would engage and reassure them they wouldn't be in the shot politely. Then the Education Director chimed in with a joke and the guards would return with a jovial response foreign to me. I was a fly on the wall to this "normal" interaction. Never once did any of them look at me, much less ask what was going on. I was completely invisible.

Emily knew these uncomfortable and awkward exchanges were the price to pay for being able to support us in any meaningful way. The irony is that these photos are used to humanize me and to let the world know I exist – that I am more than the worst thing I've done.

Invisibility is such a manifold concept as it pertains to an artist because of the desire to show one's work. Do you feel like you've achieved a healthy balance of recognition without being too recognizable? Do you have enough control over the social functions of your craft? Prison has intensified my desire to be seen, mostly because of the inherent shame.

Is it because I have something to prove? Is it about the craft or work or celebrity? Simply a restoration of dignity or a path of purpose? When invisibility is used as a weapon as opposed to a shield, it converts the spirit of the thing and the dynamic pivots. This bleeds into what André 3000 says about social anxiety and how it couples with artistry. The most profound art is generated out of the depths of a personal place, then becomes an entity in its own right thus developing a different layer of function that requires a social aspect or nuance. Maybe it's all a cycle: the social anxiety initiates the introspection that inspires the work, which increases the visibility that feeds the social anxiety that fuels more work or breaks the process. André 3000 has transcended his nature and used its disfunction as a tool. I've been thinking about that a lot lately, given the polarization of our nation. Every group that ripples out from me seems to perpetuate this unwillingness to empathize with those they oppose: inmates, guards, staff, the public, etc. Most seem to be stuck within their own perceptions, never questioning their unconscious bias. I'm trying to be more aware of my natural parameters: my critical nature, my preachy tone, holding people to unrealistic standards and my inclination to prove my point at an unnecessary expense. Do you think it is a noble effort to challenge our personal nature?

Man Alec, those words you sent from *Invisible Man* gave me goosebumps. They are so universal and timeless. They represent the complexity of "the dark" so eloquently. These places, Rush City specifically, are ruled by hate, they fuel an antagonistic spirit that threatens to break us down without the love necessary to build us back up. Prison isn't supposed to be a place of light; the expectation is dark because of the retributive purpose these places serve. Yet that is not what I want to personify. It is not the justice Cornell West spoke of that is rooted in love.

I was just reading a poetry review where a Queer/Trans poet spoke about the expectation of having to only write about the darkness of their pain and suffering served as a misguided function. Cameron Awkward-Rich said, "Queer/Trans sorrow are often consumed in ways that reinforce these systems rather than disrupt them." I am hypersensitive about how the incarcerated artist is projected. Knowing that you see me separate from this place and these circumstances affirms to me that the darkness was a necessary part of the journey. I am realizing that my eyes have adjusted to being able to see in the most minimal light and there is now a peaceful partnership at play. I sink into myself, grapple with the pain, listen to music, read poetry, write or draw – then convert that energy into a tangible symbol of dignity – undeniably. I carry the darkness as a privilege and see it as a responsibility to find a way to pay forward with purpose.

Okay, man. Again, great to hear your voice, my friend. I'll contact you when I figure out what's going on around here & maybe we can schedule another call next week. I do wonder if we'll get those Covid results & just disappear on quarantine?

Be well my friend,

Much Love & Respect…

8.6.20

Hi Chris,

It was so great that you called while I was at Kathy's with Char – like it was meant to be! I was going to surprise you with the picture I made, but it was even better that you called.

Hope the COVID shit hasn't gone crazy there and you are doing okay.

Take care, my friend,
Alec

8.9.20

Hey Alec,

Allow me to shatter the fourth wall a bit to add context and speak on the serendipity of our last few encounters. The night after we first talked on the phone, the guards came by and asked if I wanted to volunteer for kitchen duty in the morning. So the next morning, I woke up at 3:30 am, had a cup of coffee, then worked a grueling 13 and 1/2 hour shift. After a shower, I decided to call Kathy to fill them in on what's going on. The house phone just rang. For a second I contemplated calling someone else, or just going to relax because I'd have to go back to work in the morning. I decided to call Kathy's cell. I can't tell you how harsh it's been through the years attempting to get my people together to meet/mingle with family: girlfriends, prison brothers who've been released, Char, etc. I finally realized how odd it was for me to force any sort of olive branch without me there. So hearing Char's voice on Kathy's cell phone, them saying you were there and to hear such a jovial tinge to Kathy's voice put the biggest smile on my face. It was so great to know you were all there at the same time. For a second or two I felt free, like maybe I was just running a little late to the party but am on my way. I hold on to that couple of seconds by faith.

A lot of little things needed to happen for me to be able to call at that time. I've been sitting on SHU (segregated housing unit) with only an hour out a day for seven months. If I would've turned down that kitchen job, then I wouldn't have been able to call at that specific time. I know it's a minor thing to most, given speed and accessibility to communication these days, but any tangible momentum in the joint is hard to come by. Thank you for getting all of that together. I'm so grateful I got to be a part of the experience in real time.

My apologies for the lapse in writing. There is so much great stuff I'd like to address from the last letter. I'm just kind of stuck right now in the kitchen. It's a mixed bag of blessing and a test of will. I'm on nine days straight of work and forced overtime. Many men didn't make it after a few days. They simply couldn't get out of bed in the morning and got laid off and put on the worst status of punishment for quitting. The best we could get was a couple of days with regular 8-hour shifts but no days off. It is the epitome of an essential worker. We work with kitchen support staff all day then get back to the unit only to get treated like shit by security staff. A lot of guys took the maltreatment as an opportunity to start shit and try to get a protest started. If we'd all just refuse to work, they said, we'd show them. But peaceful protests in oppressive prisons don't work without strong and co-ordinated support from the streets. To me, it boils down to my word more than anything. I said I'd work and that's what I'm going to do. Not for them but for us, because the fellas need to eat, and the machine must be oiled. If we aren't willing to go all the way, there is no point in bluffing people who don't care about us in the first place.

They put me as utility in the inventory area, dry goods and the walk-in freezer. I manage the incoming product orders and distribute the goods as needed. On my first day we got a big delivery. Now mind you, I've been laying around in a cell for seven months on 22-hour lockdown a day. Now I'm processing palettes of boxes ranging from 30-50lbs frozen foods to 20lbs of cereal/chips on shelves and crates of bread. By the second day, my forearms were as swollen as a pregnant woman's ankles, my feet were blistered and throbbing, and my back was a sneeze away from going out. But who would I be to quit? Friday I unloaded my 3rd truck shipment. Just today I sliced up 300lbs of meat. The other day I cooked 1000 servings of cabbage and a few people applauded.

Okay Alec. I just wanted to give you a quick update. I've got more coming about invisibility, fashion, style & tattooing in the next letter now that the swelling has gone down.

I pray all is well & you are in good spirits.

Much Love

8.11.20

Dear Chris,

It's been over a week since I visited Kathy's, and I'm still basking in the memory. I'm also still waiting for the film to get processed (it's an old kind of film that can't be developed in Minnesota any more), so let me just tell you about it. After you and I talked on the phone for the first time, I got up the nerve to call Kathy. I didn't want to bug her, but there was a picture I wanted to take. It goes back to the photo you imagined taking to a desert island. You described it as being a summer day on Kathy and Steve's farm "that'd capture the scope of the place while everyone is outside." I told Kathy about this idea and asked if I could also invite Char. They both agreed.

At the pond in the back of the property there's a picnic table. I had everyone gather around it, but didn't want them to pose, so I brought a deck of cards for them to play with. I also had Kathy bring down some photos for everyone to look at. As a nod to your other desert island picture, I also brought a life-size cardboard cutout of Demi Lovato, which cracked everyone up.

You talked about keeping the figures in the picture small, "more of a figurative touch," you said, so I photographed from a ladder and at a distance. After taking those pictures, I also made a close-up of the table. It was such a crazy scene when you called: me on the ladder hovering over the table, kids playing underneath, Demi in the background, your voice in the air. It was like one of those moments of inexplicable connection you have during a vivid dream.

When you talked about the experience of being photographed by Emily, you asked me about my process and how I handle the often anxiety-producing space between myself and my subject. My answer, I guess, is to accept that space — accept the strangeness. Staring into someone's eyes is like looking at the ocean. "How do you coax out that shot you know is there looming under the surface?" you asked. I can climb on ladders and coax all day, but I'll never see what's on the ocean's floor. All I can do is look for beauty in the mystery.

That reminds me, after finishing *Invisible Man,* I tracked down a couple of tangentially related publications. One was a 1952 issue of *Life* magazine in which his collaborator Gordon Parks made photographs illustrating *Invisible Man.* One picture shows the protagonist's face poking out from a manhole cover. Another shows his underground lair illuminated with dozens of lightbulbs. While I love Gordon Parks (who incidentally started his photo career in the Twin Cities), I find these pictures unsuccessful. They betray the mystery of the unnamed narrator by describing both his face and his ocean floor.

Far more interesting, to me, is one of Ellison's own photographs I found in another book. Ellison was never a professional photographer, but after meeting Parks, he became a serious amateur. In the late 40s he took a picture of a Black woman being forcibly restrained by police. The picture isn't technically perfect — the policemen are blurry and there's a flare of light in one corner. On top of that, the only existing print has a big tear in it. But all of these snapshot qualities only heighten the intensity of what is happening. The woman herself is sharply seen. You can see that she has a missing tooth and a scar on her forehead. Ellison made this woman and her struggle visible in a way that feels authentic.

I also read a book of letters between Ellison and his friend Albert Murray in which Ellison often shares his passion for photography. "I'm glad as hell to hear that you've taken up Photography;" Ellison writes in 1956 while doing a residency at the American Academy in Rome, "it's dam well time that those curious eyes of yours went on record."

Describing his attraction to photography, Ellison writes, "You know me, I have to have something between me and reality when I'm dealing with it most intensely."

Wishing you strength as you toil away in the kitchen. I'm clapping for you...

Alec

8.17.20

Hey Alec,

After 16 straight days, 14 of which were 13½ hour shifts, I finally have a day off. I intend to give you a call later, but I figured I'd type out a little message in the spirit of camaraderie.

I'm just glad to have some space to write you. Only I have to share this space with another dude, one who doesn't feel it's a necessity to clean the room or stop talking about himself. So it's not like I can retreat into my art or writing like I used to at Stillwater. I'm more comfortable in my own head, with my own thoughts or with my work. Maybe that's what being an artist is all about, processing through the medium because it doesn't convey any other way.

Talk to you soon…

Much love & respect,

8.24.20

Dear Chris,

So great to hear your voice yesterday. It's too bad I can't send you posters of the farm pics. But I came up with the idea of cutting them up in sections, so they'd fit in a regular envelope. Let me know if they make it to you.

Lots of love,
Alec

Acknowledgements

First & foremost, I must acknowledge everyone who has been negatively impacted by my actions, rippling out of a brokenness I completely own. I know words can never be enough; please know that I carry you within my heart as I confront an insurmountable debt & search for ways to pay it forward. I'll never forget how much I owe humanity.

My immense gratitude to Alec, for taking a chance on responding to my initial letter: Your openness, your friendship & your investment in this project has changed the trajectory of life for me my friend. I look forward to continuing our dialogue & will forever appreciate your presence.

A special thanks to Michael Mack, who saw value in our conversation & took a chance on publishing it.

I am an amalgamation of so many wonderful people who have come, gone & stuck around throughout all my turmoil. To those who didn't give up on me & who have kept in touch despite the numerous reasons to move on: I hope you can hear the appreciation I have for you in my voice every time we speak — much love. To those I haven't talked to in a while: I miss you & hope you are well. To those who've moved on, I understand & apologize for letting you down. To those I've met during my incarceration who see me for who I am today & support me regardless of my circumstance, thank you.

To all my Brothers who've been bidding with me, who've taught me how to grow in the darkness & shine without light; I love ya'll & won't stop until we're all free!

To my extended family of artists who span genre & medium across the spectrum of voice, who inspire me to speak every word through various languages, thank you.

Thank you to all those who are allowing me to earn back my voice by listening to me. You qualify my future by not discrediting my words based on my atrocious past. Thank you for being bold enough to not only continue to carry on the conversation, but also to manifest your integrity in action & deed. We don't need permission to make decisions that are confirmed in our heart. Don't second guess, don't question, don't doubt what you know to be true & righteous. And don't hesitate to reach out to people, you never know what may transpire. To those I have yet to meet, I'm looking forward to hearing from you.

To my fellow fallen: incarceration is where we hone our character despite the damage of the DOC's current governing mentality. Take hold of your future by confronting your past. You are better than your greatest mistake, you are better than the way they treat you; please continue to fight the good fight & prove it. No matter what they say, no matter what they do, don't let it dictate your behavior in any way that doesn't motivate you to discover the best version of yourself. You got this!

At the risk of being too presumptuous, I will be more specific in the acknowledgments of my next project. There are so many individuals to honor, consider it an act of faith to say I got an extensive list on its way. Much love...

— C. Fausto Cabrera

It wasn't long ago that I received my first letter from C. Fausto Cabrera, but in the months since, the world has been turned upside down. Chris's friendship has been a buoy, his perspective a lodestar. I can't imagine getting through this year without him. It's been a pleasure meeting a few of Chris's loved ones. Thanks to Kathy and Steve for letting me visit their beautiful farm and to Char for her warmth and honesty. I look forward to the day when Chris can meet my family: Rachel, Carmen & Gus, Mom & Dad, and the Andersons. Thanks to the friends and colleagues who've helped with this book: Ethan, Frish, Kate, Sam, Tash, and Vince. Special thanks to Michael Mack and Morgan Crowcroft-Brown for their responsiveness. Everything about this book has been a reminder of the generous creative spirit that resists being stomped out by the hardness of the world.

— Alec Soth

Image credits: page 28 Jayson Bimber, page 29 Aaron Maurer,
page 30 Elle White, page 31 Tom Archer, page 32 James Whitty

First edition published by MACK

© 2020 MACK for this edition
© 2020 C. Fausto Cabrera & Alec Soth for their texts and images

Design by Alec Soth & Morgan Crowcroft-Brown
Copy edit by Jenny Fisher
Printed in Italy

ISBN 978-1-913620-15-8
mackbooks.co.uk